To Grandma,

Much Love from,

David & Sue

Elizabeth Andruchow

Popular Plants

Popular Plants

MARSHALL CAVENDISH

This edition published exclusively for
Coles in Canada by Marshall Cavendish
Books (a division of Marshall Cavendish
Partworks Limited)
119 Wardour Street
London W1V 3TD

© Marshall Cavendish 1993
ISBN 1 85435 568 6

Printed in Singapore

Contents

Introduction

One of the greatest of all pleasures is that of seeing a garden which you have planted and tended yourself burst into bloom in spring. A thriving garden is ample reward for the hours of toil which have gone into it over the preceding months. Equally, a garden full of miserable, wilting plants can be a depressing sight.

Making a success of your garden requires an understanding of each plant's individual characteristics and needs. Just as each is unique in appearance, so it has a particular set of conditions it needs in order to thrive. Some plants grow better in bright sunlight, others in shade. Some can be planted from seed, others will have to be bought as bulbs or already-growing plants.

Some plants will thrive if grown in large numbers in a bed while others are best as border plants or grown indoors in containers. Some will survive a frosty winter; others will not. Some are best suited to humid climates while others can cope in a dry soil.

If you understand the unique needs of each plant, the chances are your garden will thrive. In order to care for your plants

properly, you need to have the appropriate information available at your fingertips, which is where this book comes in.

Popular Plants is a reference guide to many well-liked garden plants, with an emphasis on flowers. It is intended to

help you choose the right plants for your garden's conditions, and to care for them properly. Plants covered in the book range from sunny favourites such as daffodils, marigolds, pansies and sunflowers to elegant classics such as carnations and roses. Each chapter contains a detailed description of the appearance of a particular plant, including information on the large number of varieties and sub-species available. This is accompanied by advice on what garden style – formal or informal – each is suited to. A detailed explanation is provided of

Introduction *(continued)*

the conditions each plant needs to thrive; how and when is best to plant; how to take care of the plant; and what diseases it is susceptible to.

Popular Plants is designed to be relevant to a wide range of locations and climates. Seasons, rather than specific times of year, are referred to. Readers are advised to adjust their planting schedules in accordance with local conditions.

Popular Plants is part of the *Easy Gardening* series. Other volumes in the series include *Easy Gardening*, *Creative Gardening*, *Gardening on a Small Scale* and *Gardening Techniques*.

Daffodils

Easy to grow, quick to multiply and available in an astonishing variety of enchanting spring flowers, the popular and colourful daffodil earns its place in a garden of any size.

With their brilliant golden cups, daffodils are the star of the narcissus family, the most popular of all the spring-flowering bulbs. Every garden has a place for one of the many varieties, whether tall, large-cupped and stately, or small and delicately nodding.

The growing cycle

Daffodil bulbs start their growing period in the autumn and continue slowly throughout the winter months. By spring, their foliage emerges above ground, just ahead of the crowning flowers.

After flowering, daffodils form seed pods while the bulbs go into a period of replenishment, replacing nutrients. They also multiply, producing 'bulblets', which eventually develop into full-size bulbs.

In early summer the daffodil's long, narrow leaves die down and the plant takes a rest until autumn.

Sunshine colours

The flower head consists of a trumpet or cup (the *corona*), surrounded by petals (the *perianth segments*). Some varieties of daffodil have double cups – a cup within a cup – or many layers of petals.

Yellow is the most common colour, from pale to dark, but there are also white daffodils,

Narcissi or daffodils are seen at their best when growing naturally in drifts or large clumps in grass (right).
The gloriously bright yellow daffodil 'Golden Harvest' (inset) grows up to 45cm/18in tall.

and other varieties with two separate colours – yellow and orange, white and yellow, or white and orange. Pink and white varieties are relative newcomers to the host of mainstream varieties and because of this they are more expensive to buy.

Daffodils come in various heights, from miniatures or dwarfs, just 8–15cm/4–6in tall, to the tallest varieties of regal trumpet daffodils which may reach 50cm/20in. There are masses of varieties to choose from, and these fall into the following main groupings:

Trumpet daffodils are among the most popular. Each flower has a long, prominent cup; most are yellow, but there are also many other white varieties.

Large-cupped daffodils are tall, like trumpet daffodils, growing up to 50cm/20in. Each flower has a cup-shaped centre, generally in a colour that contrasts strikingly with the petals: for instance, an orange cup surrounded by yellow petals.

Double daffodils are blooms which consist of many petals, or have a double cup, and come in a range of colours, including yellow, and combinations of yellow and white. These are also tall-growing daffodils, topping 45cm/18in.

Poeticus narcissi are valued for their very late, often sweetly scented flowers, consisting of a tiny coloured cup against white petals. These are produced on stems reaching up to 40cm/16in tall.

Triandrus narcissi are the dwarf forms, bearing clusters of drooping yellow or white flowers on stems which grow to 15–30cm/6–12in in height.

Cyclamineus narcissi are an immensely popular group

The dwarf variety 'Jumblie' (right) has delicate, 'nodding' swept-back petals. Growing to just 15–30cm/6–12in, they are less likely to topple over in fierce winds.

There are many superb double flower varieties of narcissi now available and 'Texas' (below) is a fine example, with a glowing orange tinge to its central petals.

Colourful contrasts: the white petals and creamy yellow trumpet of tall-growing 'Ice Follies' (right) serves as an excellent foil to a deeper yellow variety. 'Semper Avanti' (far right) has a classic combination of translucent white petals and vibrant gold trumpet, while tall, large-cupped 'Carlton' (below right) displays its buttery hues to the best effect in large clumps.

PLANT PROFILE

Suitable site and soil: sun or light shade; in most soils, but must be well drained.

Planting: make a hole three times the depth of the bulb.

Cultivation and care: dig in plenty of garden compost before planting. Add gravel or sand to aid drainage. After flowering, feed regularly and allow the leaves to die down.

Propagation: break off small bulblets and re-plant.

Pests and diseases: mainly trouble-free, but liable to rot in badly-drained soil.

Recommended varieties:
Tall:
Yellow
'Carlton' (large cupped)
'Dutch Master' (trumpet)
'Golden Ducat' (double)
'Golden Harvest' (trumpet)
'King Alfred' (trumpet)
'Magnificence' (trumpet)
'Unsurpassable' (trumpet)
Yellow and orange
'Fortune' (large cupped)
'Scarlet O'Hara' (large cupped)
'Texas' (double)
White
'Cheerfulness' (double)
'Mount Hood' (trumpet)
'White Lion' (double)
White and yellow
'Actaea' (poeticus)
'Flower Record' (large cupped)
'Old Pheasant Eye' (poeticus)
'Semper Avanti' (large cupped)

Miniature or dwarf:
Yellow
'February Gold' (cyclamineus)
'Jumblie' (cyclamineus)
'Liberty Bells' (triandrus)
Narcissus bulbocodium (wild)
Narcissus cyclamineus (wild)
'Peeping Tom' (cyclamineus)
'Tête-à-tête' (cyclamineus)
Yellow and orange
'March Sunshine' (cyclamineus)
'Suzy' (jonquil)
White
'February Silver' (cyclamineus)
'Jenny' (cyclamineus)
Narcissus triandrus albus (wild)
'Silver Chimes' (triandrus)
'Thalia' (triandrus)
White and yellow
'Jack Snipe' (cyclamineus)
'Dove Wings' (cyclamineus)
'Little Beauty' (trumpet)

that consist mainly of dwarf varieties (15–30cm/6–12in) derived from the wild species, *Narcissus cyclamineus*. These boast the highly distinctive flowers of the species: long trumpets and swept-back petals, which give the impression that they are facing into a strong wind. The flowers are yellow or white or bi-coloured.

Jonquils have sweetly fragrant clusters of yellow or white flowers and grow up to 15–30cm/6–12in high.

Buying bulbs

Garden centres offer a good range of varieties, but if you want a wider choice buy from a specialist bulb grower. They sell by mail order and supply

well-illustrated catalogues.

For the maximum number of flowers buy the largest bulbs available of that particular species and variety. Choose your bulbs as soon as they appear in the shops; if left for too long on the shelves they will deteriorate. Avoid any with blemishes, loose outer skins or softness around the base where the roots will show. This usually means the bulbs have been displayed in conditions that are too warm.

Getting the best effect

The taller-growing daffodils make excellent cut flowers so, if you have enough space, rather than spoil your main garden display, grow a row specially for cutting. They will

grow virtually anywhere, so you need not worry about providing exactly the right sort of conditions. They do thrive, however, in sun or light shade.

For the best effect daffodils should be planted boldly in drifts or groups of irregular shape. The miniature and dwarf varieties look particularly effective in rock gardens, between paving stones or at the front of mixed borders.

The taller-growing daffodils look best planted near shrubs, particularly spring-flowering kinds such as deutzia, forsythia, flowering currant (ribes), magnolias and camellias.

Natural attraction

Daffodils look very attractive growing in lawns, especially in clumps under a tree. You can use any type, but especially recommended are the poeticus, trumpet and large-cupped varieties.

You can use daffodils for spring bedding but, in this case, you must lift the bulbs after flowering and replant them elsewhere to make way for summer bedding plants.

Trumpet, large-cupped and double daffodils are best for spring bedding. Grow them in bold groups with blue forget-me-nots and polyanthus.

Preparing the site

Daffodils will grow in a wide range of soils but the site must be well drained, as the bulbs are liable to rot if the soil is wet or waterlogged over the winter months.

Dig the ground thoroughly before planting, adding very well-rotted manure or garden compost. If the drainage is poor then mix plenty of coarse

PROJECT PLANTING IN GRASS

To plant narcissus bulbs in a lawn or rough grass, scatter them gently in the area. This creates a more natural look, as you can plant the bulbs almost where they land. Using a bulb planter, make a hole for the bulb to almost three times its depth. If the bulb is planted in more shallow soil, it is less likely to flower well and naturalize – produce new bulblets. Put a little sand in the base of the hole and set the bulb in firmly, making sure there are no air pockets beneath. Add some peat and a sprinkling of bone meal to give the bulb a good start, then return the soil to the hole. Press down firmly and water the area well.

PERFECT PARTNERS

Create striking spring bedding arrangements by using creamy pale narcissi to offset vivid-coloured, low growing perennials. Here, Narcissus poeticus 'Actaea' harmonizes with the vibrant blue and yellow of polyanthus 'Crescendo Blue'.

'Jack Snipe' (below) a small white and yellow Cyclamineus narcissus, is one that naturalizes well in small corners. A sturdy variety, which grows to 23cm/9in, it flowers in early to mid-spring. The creamy white petals are distinctively swept back from its narrow, lemon-coloured cup.

sand or grit into the soil.

At planting time, apply a sprinkling of bone meal mixed with peat, which releases food to the bulbs slowly over the winter.

Buy the bulbs when you are ready to plant them, ideally in late summer or early autumn. When planting in informal groups or drifts, scatter the bulbs on the ground first and then plant them where they fall (within reason). This gives a natural, clumped look. Space large daffodils 10–20cm/4–8in apart and dwarf and miniature varieties about 8cm/3in apart.

The depth of the planting varies according to the size of the bulb. The largest bulbs should be set into 15cm/6in deep holes, the smallest into 8cm/3in holes.

Planting tips

Dig your bulb holes with a hand trowel or with a special bulb planter. This neat gadget takes out a core of soil, then replaces it when the bulb has been set in the hole. It is essential that each bulb sits firmly at the bottom of the hole because if there is a gap the bulb may fail to root and grow.

After planting, water the area thoroughly, especially if the soil is dry. Bulbs will not start growing in dry conditions.

For the future . . .

Remove dead flowerheads to prevent the plant setting seed. After flowering, feed the soil around the remaining foliage with a general-purpose liquid fertilizer. This ensures a good flower display the following year. Give two or three feeds at weekly or fortnightly intervals, first making sure the soil is moist so that the fertilizer is absorbed efficiently.

Allow the leaves to die down completely before cutting them back as they replace all the nutrients taken out of the bulbs with flowering. If grown in grass, do not mow the area of lawn around the bulbs until the foliage has withered, nor tie the leaves together.

Carnations and Pinks

These charming summer flowers are a must for any flower arranger, so fill your borders with their colourful blooms and delicious perfume.

Carnations and pinks belong to the same family: *Dianthus*. Most species smell delicious and – particularly in the case of pinks – are essential to the easy informality of the cottage-style garden.

They will grow happily in most soils and are tolerant of salt spray and smoke pollution. They are comparatively trouble-free and on the whole succumb only to the usual garden pests such as greenfly, which are easily dealt with.

One of their biggest attractions is their use as a cut flower. They look good in flower arrangements and last well – and they are a popular choice for buttonholes.

Gardeners' choice
Only 'border' carnations will grow out of doors. Every year beautiful new colours, sizes and shapes appear on the market but it is as well to remember that hybridization (the crossing of parent plants to produce a new variety) tends to remove any perfume. If you are the type of gardener who is more interested in old-fashioned nostalgia than the horticultural competition of growing something nobody else has – do ask about a variety's scent before you buy.

Carnations and pinks have interesting attributes not always obvious to the beginner. The foliage of carnations and pinks is a gentle but outstanding grey-green, which will enhance borders even when the flowers have died.

Best buys
Carnations and pinks are very easy to propagate, although growing them from seed is not very easy. It is best to buy a few young plants from garden

The rounded flowers of the dwarf Alpine pink, Dianthus alpinus (left), grow 10cm/4in above a compact green, spiky-leaved mat. With varieties ranging in colour from rose-pink to crimson, this delightful pink is perfect for any border. It is especially suited to humus-rich soil.

All garden pinks have a delightfully old-fashioned feel and are ideal for borders with an informal, country flavour. They mix well with many different cottage-garden plants, such as blue-mauve Aquilegia vulgaris (right).

Pinks and carnations are, understandably, a great favourite with gardeners. The white feathery petals of 'Mrs Sinkins' (above) is just one fine example of the wide variety of shapes and colours that make pinks ideal for an unusual garden display.

centres or by mail order. Best results are obtained in full sun with plenty of light and air. They can be planted in autumn or spring but spring is better if you are a beginner because you may be reluctant to face going outside on a cold, wet winter's day just to make sure that your new plants are becoming established.

CUT FLOWERS

If your garden is small, you may not like to cut flowers from it for the house. Carnations and pinks, however, will renew themselves so prolifically that a bunch taken here and there will not be noticeable. Nothing is prettier than a clutch of pinks in an old-fashioned china pot. Remove their lower leaves or they will rot. Change the water every four days, add a proprietary flower preserver and try to keep them out of strong sunlight.

Carnations are not as easy as pinks to use as cut flowers. Change the water every four days and follow these simple instructions:
- Cut carnations at the end of a sunny day
- Chop stems diagonally – don't squash them
- Stand flowers up to their necks in water overnight
- Keep flowers in a cool place and not near tomatoes, apples or bananas which give off ethylene gas and can kill them within a day.
- Do not mix them with anything else. They look better on their own in the vase, as they do in the garden, although white gypsophila does not detract too much.

If your plants arrive dry, they should be watered and allowed to drain. Space them about 38cm/15in apart so that there is room for them to form compact beds in their second year. When planting carnations – which look good and survive best in a bed of their own – leave sufficient room between the plants to accommodate the newcomers you will be able to propagate later.

Add a little organic bonemeal to the hole and bury only the roots, keeping the lower leaves and stems completely free of soil. Then water them in (without drowning them). Check after a couple of days if the soil has shrunk away from the roots. If it has, firm it very gently back.

Splendid isolation

Carnations are happier and look better in a bed of their own. 'Border' types will grow easily in the garden but they do not like being swamped by lush neighbours in a herbaceous border because this can prevent light and air reaching their leaves. They are a bit too rigid for patio pots but they can look wonderful in a sunny, well-drained corner in a choice of colours mixed together.

There are three main groups. Selfs, as their name suggests, are all one colour. Picotees are usually either white or yellow, edged with a contrast. Varieties known as 'flakes' or 'bizarres' are multi-coloured, spotted or streaked. This last type is difficult to find and does not 'marry in' well with the other two. Avoid them unless you really want to impress your neighbours!

A somewhat newer and really spectacular carnation is the Tyrolean trailing type. Unlike the others it is quite happy to share its home with other flowers. In window boxes, in good soil and sunshine, its trailing habit will become more pronounced each season, producing large, nicely scented double flowers which go beautifully with lobelia, fuchsias or pelargoniums. Just

There is a pink to suit every situation and taste. Bushy Dianthus barbatus (above), popularly known as sweet William, is good for the middle of a border.

Double-flowered 'Pike's Pink' (right), which grows in compact fragrant cushions 10cm/4in high and across, is ideal for rock gardens.

The smart blooms of 'London Poppet' (below) make it an excellent choice for formal borders, while the stunning cerise flowers of D. deltoides 'Flashing Light' (left) brighten up a quiet spot.

remember that window boxes need frequent watering in summer to make sure the compost does not get too dry.

With carnations it is particularly important to know that, unlike most other flowers, you do not feed them once the buds show colour, or they may go on to produce shapeless flowers. Feed them at weekly intervals when they have started into growth and then again when flowering has ceased until around mid-autumn. Start feeding once again the following spring, until buds show colour once more.

Helping hand

It is necessary to support carnations and the easiest way is with special hoops, either galvanized or plastic, available from garden centres.

Never 'pinch them out' or 'stop' them as they are producing all those slightly smaller flowers for your pleasure. It is such a shame to remove the flowers simply in order to get a few much larger ones which you would then have to cut in any case in order to exhibit them in a competition.

If you keep the bed weeded, you will not need to water carnations too often, except in very dry spells. Remove faded

Pinks are clump-forming in habit and flower prolifically through the summer, making them the perfect choice for the front of a border. With colours ranging from white, through all the shades of pink, to bright red, you will find one to match any colour scheme. The delicate dual colouring of the dwarf Dianthus 'Persian Carpet' (right) will complement fiery borders full of red and pink flowers.

PLANT PROFILE

Suitable site and soil: Dianthus like a situation in full sun with plenty of air. They prefer a well-drained soil and they do like lime, so ideally it should be naturally present in quantity. Try them first and then add lime if they need it.

Cultivation and care: cover only the roots, never the foliage. Keep soil moist but never water-logged. Do not feed once the buds begin to show colour.

Propagation: very quick and easy by 'layering' but simple cuttings are convenient for pinks.

Pests and diseases: only the usual ones such as greenfly – but watch out for slugs after outdoor propagation.

Recommended varieties:
Border carnations:
● Selfs – the best pure white varieties include 'Eudoxia', 'Spindrift' and 'Whitecliff'. For stunning crimsons choose 'Oscar', 'Crimson Velvet' or 'Freeland Crimson'. If you want apricot shades, pick 'Consul', 'Clunie' or 'Flameau'. Sunny yellow is an interesting option and 'Aldridge Yellow', 'Beauty of Cambridge' and 'Brimstone' are the best. Traditional pink blooms are always popular and 'Frances Sellars', 'Bookham Peach' and 'Cherry Clove' are very reliable. 'Lavender Clove', 'Lord Grey' and 'Clarabelle' are among the best of the lavender shades.

● In Picotees the following give an impressive display. 'Alice Forbes' is white with rosy mauve markings. 'Catherine Glover' is yellow edged with scarlet. 'Harmony' is French grey with pink stripes. 'Horsa' is apricot with scarlet markings.

Pinks
● For the best old-fashioned pinks choose from the following. 'Earl of Essex' is pink with fringed petals. 'Mrs Sinkins' is heavily scented in pink or white. 'Sam Barlow' is a serrated double white bloom with an almost black eye. 'Show Beauty' is deep rose with a maroon eye. 'Priory Pink' is bluish mauve.

● There are lots of varieties of modern pinks. 'Doris' is a beautiful pale pink with a red eye and many other pinks are related. 'Doris Majestic' is salmon pink and 'Doris Supreme' is pale pink with carmine flakes and stripes. 'London Delight' is mauve with a purple eye and 'Haytor White' is pure white.

● Alpine pinks are generally small and suitable for growing in paving, walls or in rockeries. 'Mars' is bright crimson, 'Pike's Pink' is a heavily fringed pale pink double with a cerise centre and 'Musgrave's Pink' is white with a green eye. For a miniature rock dianthus try 'Hollycroft Fragrance' which is pink with a dark centre.

SIMPLY DIVINE

Nobody really knows where the three hundred or more species of carnations, pinks and sweet Williams which make up the dianthus family originated. The name itself comes from the Greek 'dios anthos' which means 'divine flower'. This is a most appropriate description for such a delightful, widely varying family and is specially true of carnations.

The elegant blooms of border and perpetual carnations, such as double-flowered 'Valencia' (left), make excellent cut flowers and are popular when made up as buttonholes. Large blooms are produced by pinching out all but the main bud on each stem.

No matter how small your garden, there is always room for a dianthus plant somewhere. Here, 'Queen of Hearts' (below) provides a splash of bright crimson amongst the green foliage.

blooms about halfway down the stem and, when flowering is finished altogether, cut back all the long stems.

Pretty in pink

Pinks are not necessarily pink but come in many shades from pure white through to deep red. Some have a contrasting 'eye'. Others, known as 'laced', have sport coloured edges.

Old-fashioned pinks flower only once in summer but they make thickly-spreading mats, useful as ground cover to smother weeds or to droop over the hard edges of new rockeries. They are invaluable planted as 'pockets' to soften the severe look of paving slabs or crazy paving.

The best-known 'maiden pink' (*Dianthus deltoides*) has little perfume and its leaves are bright green rather than grey. It bears drifts of single deep pink flowers from early summer until autumn. For perfume try the pure white 'Mrs Sinkins', which has the inherent 'clove' scent typical of the dianthus family.

For colour and even more variety, the beginner should look for modern pinks. These popular blooms resemble old-fashioned pinks but are larger in flower, less compact and mat-forming and they bloom throughout the summer and into autumn. They are known

SLUGS

Young pinks and carnations are a great favourite with slugs. To protect your new plants after planting them out in the garden, cover them with improvised cloches made from large plastic lemonade bottles. Cut the bottoms off and place them over the plants, without their screw tops.

KEEPING CARNATIONS TALL AND STRAIGHT

Carnations grow tall – on average to 60cm/2ft and sometimes even higher – supporting their wonderful blooms on long, elegant stems. As a result the plants generally need a little help to keep them upright and to encourage their stems to grow straight. This applies to all types of carnation, whether planted out in the border or grown in pots in a greenhouse. Young plants can easily be supported with a stake and wire hoop which you can make yourself or buy. As the plants grow taller continue to support them.

1 *Push a stake into the ground behind each plant; take care not to damage the roots.*

2 *Loop a length of light gauge wire, around, twisting the two ends together.*

Low-growing pinks fill the gap between taller plants and the edge of this informal border (above).

Edging a border, delicate pinks tone in with aubrieta and Muscari plumosa 'Monstrosum' (below).

as 'perpetual' but that does not mean they flower in winter.

Modern pinks are all descended from the famous Allwoodii hybrid which was produced by crossing an old-fashioned pink with a perpetual-flowering carnation. The popular 'Doris' was one of the first – it has fragrant salmon pink flowers with a reddish eye, and sometimes blooms on into winter, making it a welcome cut flower. 'Doris' has quite a few relatives: 'Doris Supreme', 'Doris Elite', 'Doris Majestic' and 'Doris Ruby', for instance, all of which have inherited the variety's good points being hardy, trouble-free, perfumed and prolific.

A group known as *Dianthus allwoodii alpinus* forms clumps about a foot in diameter and is perfect for rockeries, stone walls and paths.

Planting places

The modern pink, with its hardiness and long flowering period, will enhance almost any part of your garden design. Grouped on a sunny bank, around a sundial, bird table or patio pot, or even in sink gardens, its contrasting colours make bright and lasting splashes of colour.

In a small bedding scheme, however, use only one or two varieties as edging and plant them well apart to give them room to develop. Then plant miniature bulbs of iris, hyacinth, daffodil, dog's tooth violet or lily of the field in between for spring colour before your pinks appear.

Sweet Peas

No wonder the sweet pea is such a garden favourite. It produces flowers by the armful and the more you pick, the more the flowers appear.

Next to roses, sweet peas must be one of the most popular of all garden flowers. Perhaps this is because they are easy to grow and produce masses of blooms all summer with a minimum of care and attention. Many have a delicious, strong fragrance while some are only lighty scented. All are suitable for cutting.

Sweet peas are hardy annuals – the plants tolerate frosts in spring, and die at the end of the year, when the flower display is over. Most are climbers and support themselves with curly shoots known as tendrils, but some are very short plants, known as 'dwarfs', which need no form of support.

Delightfully delicate
The flowers are distinctive, having one large upright petal and two wing-like petals. The range of sweet pea colours is enormous: scarlet, crimson, maroon, purple, lavender, blue, pink, orange, cream and white. You can buy named varieties in single colours or mixtures of colours.

Sweet peas are generally bought as seeds and the biggest selection is offered by mail-order. A more limited range is available from garden centres. You should also be able to buy young plants from garden centres in the spring, as an alternative to raising your own plants from seeds.

Another reason why sweet peas are so popular is that they can be grown in various parts of the garden, from containers on the patio to flower borders and even among the vegetables if you just want blooms for cutting.

All sweet peas, whether tall or dwarf, like a spot open to the sky with plenty of sun. The more sun they see, the more flowers are produced. Avoid the shade as you will not achieve the results you want. Any soil is suitable as long as it drains well and does not become waterlogged after rain.

Apart from this do not worry too much about the soil as sweet peas are adaptable. Do ensure that they receive plenty of water: some soils dry out faster than others, particularly those containing a high proportion of sand, gravel and chalk, so take special care with these.

The right soil
If sweet peas have a preference, it is for slightly limy or chalky soil. They like a deep cool soil if at all possible and this can be achieved by digging in plenty of bulky organic matter before sowing or planting. Moist peat, well-rotted

Drops of rain from a summer shower glisten on the delicate petals of this spectacular display of sweet peas (above). The colours blend in complete harmony, ranging from crimson to lilac and white to peach. Keep tall sweet peas tied in to tall stakes at the back of a border or even in the vegetable patch (right).

garden compost, or one of the new peat substitutes such as coconut fibre will do the trick. The latter are a bit more expensive than peat but highly recommended if you want to become a 'green gardener'.

Choosing between tall and dwarf varieties should be no problem as you can obtain both types from garden

PLANT PROFILE

Suitable site and soil: Choose an open position with plenty of sun. Any well-drained soil will do.

Planting: young plants can be planted in the garden or in containers when about 10cm/4in high, during spring. Space them 15-20cm/6-8in apart.

Cultivation and care: dig in plenty of garden compost, peat or a peat substitute before planting. Pinch out tips of plants when they are about 10cm/4in high to ensure plenty of side shoots. Water regularly, especially during dry weather. Feed plants every seven to ten days during summer with a general-purpose or flower-garden liquid fertilizer. Dead-head regularly. Discard when flowering is over.

Propagation: Sow seeds in spring. They can be sown directly into the ground or containers, 12mm/½in deep and 15-20cm/6-8in apart. Alternatively seeds can be sown in seed trays, using a soil-less or John Innes seed compost. Place the tray on a cool sill indoors or in a sheltered spot in the garden.

Pests and diseases: Sweet peas are prone to slugs and snails so scatter slug pellets around them. Greenfly can be a problem and are found in the shoots tips; spray with a proprietary greenfly killer.

Recommended varieties:
Dwarf sweet peas are available in mixed colours. 'Bijou' is particularly weather resistant. 'Jet Set' is particularly fragrant and carries large waved flowers in bright colours on long stems. 'Patio' is a lightly fragrant variety and is good for beds and borders.

Tall sweet peas are available in single or mixed colours. White or cream varieties include the fragrant 'Royal Wedding'. 'Swan Lake' is good for cut flowers and looks good in beds too. 'White Leamington' is pure white and sweetly scented. Scarlet sweet peas include the fragrant 'Air Warden', excellent in borders and will add a splash of colour to your flower arrangements. 'Winston Churchill' is a bright crimson variety.

'Air Warden' (above) is an annual which grows up to 3m/10ft. The cerise-scarlet flowers are sure to create a sensation.

For a more delicate look go for one of the many pink varieties of sweet pea. Sugary-pink, salmon-pink, peachy-pink... the choice is endless.

Dwarf sweet peas need no support and come in many striking colours like this brilliant red (below).

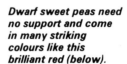

PREPARING SEEDS

Sweet pea seeds have an extremely hard coating on the outside and this can delay germination. To speed up the process, soak the seeds in water for 12 hours before sowing, to soften them. Alternatively nick the seeds with a sharp knife, or rub them in one place with glasspaper, just enough to remove a small part of the seed coat and allow moisture to enter when sown.

centres and all major seed catalogues will contain a selection of each variety. The least trouble to grow are the smallest dwarf kinds as they do not require supports.

Tall varieties may be 1.8m/ 6ft and even up to 3m/10ft high. These are excellent for planting towards the back of a flower border. The tall varieties produce more flowers than the dwarfs, so are a better choice if armfuls of cut flowers are what you want.

Support systems

There are various ways of supporting tall sweet peas. In the flower border you could put up a 1.8m/6ft high wigwam of thick bamboo canes secured at the top with a plastic cane-support ring. The stems can be secured quickly and easily with wire plant rings.

Some of the most attractive-looking supports for sweet peas which are to be grown in

PERFECT PARTNERS

A beautiful combination in a mixed border consists of dwarf sweet peas grown in conjunction with tall white foxgloves, with their decorative bell-shaped flowers. The rose-mauve flowers of foxglove *Digitalis* × *mertonensis* would also look effective in this group.

a flower border are tall twiggy sticks. Tree pruning and cutting down large shrubs provide a good supply of sticks. They can be inserted in a circle in the border and the sweet peas planted or sown around the edge.

To form a colourful screen at the back of a border you may prefer to grow sweet peas on netting. Choose plastic pea and bean netting with a mesh size of 13cm/5in square, or a large-mesh wire netting. It should be 1.8m/6ft high and supported with timber posts at each end. Stretch galvanised wires between the posts and tie the netting to these.

Tall sweet peas can also be grown against sunny walls and fences (a good way of brightening up an unsightly garage wall). Support them with pea and bean netting, wire netting or trellis panels fixed to the wall or fence. If you have a trellis screen or a pergola in the garden this would also make an ideal support for sweet peas. For a spectacular effect allow them to intertwine with climbing roses.

Box of delights

Dwarf sweet peas are ideal for containers such as patio tubs and window boxes. They can also make a colourful edging to a flower border. Height ranges from 30-90cm/1-3ft depending on the variety. The shortest varieties include 'Patio' and the tallest 'Jet Set'.

The tallest of the dwarf sweet peas will benefit from a little support to ensure they remain upright. Use either twiggy sticks left over from

pruning or proprietary metal plant supports – the kind that encircle clumps of plants. Both types of support should be inserted before the plants become too tall – ideally when they are about 10cm/4in high.

Containers for dwarf sweet peas should be filled with a suitable potting compost. This can be a light-weight peat-based or soil-less type, or one of the new peat alternatives. You might prefer to use the traditional John Innes potting compost No. 1.

Regular checks

Sweet peas need plenty of water to grow well – the soil must be kept permanently moist and not allowed to dry out. You will need to check containers daily, or even twice a day in hot weather.

When watering make sure you apply enough, so that it actually runs out of the bottom of the container. Then you will know that the entire depth of compost has been moistened.

Sweet peas are great as cut flowers and freshly opened

blooms will last a long time in water in a cool room. The fragrant varieties will, of course, scent the room. In fact, you may find some of them almost overpowering! Pick the blooms with long stems early in the morning and stand them up to their necks in water for a few hours before arranging. Sweet peas do not need other plant material to enchance them, although some sprays of gypsophila in an arrangement can look very pretty.

Sweet peas need not be confined to the back of the border. Plant them beneath a window (above) where their wonderful fragrance will waft through the open window in summer. Grow them with oxalis and saxifraga for a delightful cottage garden effect.

To keep sweet peas looking lovely remove pods, seeds and dead flower heads as they appear (below).

If you grow varieties in single colours you will be able to co-ordinate your sweet pea arrangements with the colour schemes of your rooms. Cut blooms regularly to ensure continuous flowering.

In the garden sweet peas combine beautifully with many kinds of plants. They will be 'at home' in mixed borders with shrubs, perennials and other annuals. They look particularly good growing with climbing or tall shrub roses. They could be grown through a large shrub that has flowered earlier in the year and which otherwise would look dull and uninteresting throughout summer, such as a spring-flowering forsythia.

Complementary plants

Sweet peas provide a tranquil cottage garden atmosphere, especially if grown alongside flowers such as roses, delphiniums, hollyhocks, honeysuckle, sweet Williams, Canterbury bells, foxgloves and mulleins.

In a more formal garden, silver-foliage summer bedding plants like *Senecio cineraria* make a good foil for dwarf sweet peas. Grow them in containers such as tubs, window boxes and hanging baskets.

French and African Marigolds

Bring touches of gold and bronze to every corner of your garden with these long-lasting, and trouble-free annuals.

With their showy, long-lasting blooms, tidy growth habit and sturdy stems, French and African marigolds are among the most popular and easy-to-grow annuals in the yellow and orange colour range. They are equally happy in city, suburban and country gardens, and as attractive in formal bedding schemes as in informal mixed borders. They are also ideal for containers and window boxes.

In spite of their names, French and African marigolds are Mexican in origin, and are half-hardy annuals belonging to the daisy, or *Compositae*, family. They grow, according to the type and variety, from 13.5-90cm/5in-3ft high, and flower non-stop, from early summer until the first frost.

The flowers can be single and daisy-like, fully double like carnations, or have petals around a central crest. Bright yellow and orange are traditional colours, but there are vivid mahogany red and lemon yellow varieties too. Some varieties have two-toned flowers, with striped, edged or blotched petals. The dark-green, deeply divided, glossy leaves have a distinctive pungent scent when crushed.

African marigolds *(Tagetes erecta)* are also called Aztec or American marigolds. These are the real show-stoppers, with massive double yellow or orange blooms, 7.5cm-20cm/3-8in across, densely packed with petals. They have a stiff, upright habit, and are branching but not bushy.

Tall varieties, 60-90cm/2-3ft high, include 'Sovereign', with golden yellow flowers; 'Doubloon', with light yellow

The French marigold (Tagetes patula) is available in both single and double-flowered forms in either solid yellow, orange or mahogany red, or in interesting two-tone effects like this double variety 'Russet Sophia' (left) and single 'Susanna' (below).

PERFECT FOR DRYING

You can preserve the bright colour of African marigolds all year round by air drying them. Orange varieties are best. Pick when they are just fully open, on a dry, sunny day. Cut the stem short and insert a fine stub wire, available from florists, up the hollow stem and into the flower head. Bend at the top to secure, then hang in a dry, warm spot out of direct sunlight. As they dry, the flowers shrink, but the colour remains surprisingly clear.

flowers; 'Hawaii', rich orange; and 'Sierra Mixed', with light yellow, dark yellow and orange flowers. 'Giant Fluffy Mixed', ruffled and fully double, like huge chrysanthemums; and 'Toreador', with rich orange blooms, are also worth trying.

Dwarf varieties, 25-30cm/ 10-12in high, include 'Moonbeam', with very pretty pale yellow flowers. The compact, uniform, F1 hybrid 'Inca' series, available in mixed and single colours, includes 'Sunshine Mixed', 'Inca Orange' and 'Inca Gold'.

French marigolds (*T. patula*) grow 15-30cm/6-12in high, with either single, daisy-like

PLANT PROFILE

Suitable site and soil: ordinary, well-drained soil and sun are best, though fertile soil produces the biggest blooms. Dig over the soil before planting, remove all weeds and work in some well-rotted garden compost or sterilized organic compost, available in bags from garden centres.

Planting: plant out after the last frost, in late spring or early summer. A week before planting, put the trays or pots outside during the day, in a sunny, sheltered spot, to harden off the plants. (Bring them in again at night or in cold weather.)

Space dwarf varieties 20cm/8in apart, ordinary varieties 30cm/12in apart, and tall African marigolds 45cm/18in apart. Press down the soil or potting compost around the stem with your hand or the back of a trowel. Water in well.

Cultivation and care: continue watering until established, then only in long dry spells. Remove faded flowers to keep plants looking tidy and to encourage more flower buds to form. For extra large African marigold flowers, pinch off all but the top flower bud, as soon as the side buds appear. Tall varieties may need staking on exposed sites. Dig up and discard plants after the first autumn frost, since they will not bloom again.

Propagation: sow seed under glass in early or mid-spring, 6-8 weeks before the last expected spring frost. Cover the seeds lightly with seed compost. Keep at a steady temperature (18°C/64°F) and just moist; the seeds should sprout quickly. As soon as the seedlings are large enough to handle, gently transplant into trays, 5cm/2in apart in each direction, or into pots.

Pests and diseases: slugs and snails love marigolds, so use slug pellets. Botrytis, or grey mould, can attack plants in damp conditions, and can rot flower heads.

French marigolds look particularly effective planted in drifts (above) rather than dotted about singly or in groups of two or three.

If you will be looking at your marigolds from a distance, single colours tend to be most effective. If, on the other hand, you can grow some in window boxes or other containers, you will be more able to appreciate subtle colour combinations like those of this French marigold 'Bolero' (above).

The dwarf 'Inca' series of African marigolds comes in mixed and single colours, including this striking 'Inca Gold' (left).

or double flowers, often with a densely packed central 'crest'. They can be in solid colours of yellow, orange or mahogany red, or striped, splashed, mottled, edged or tinged in a contrasting colour.

Attractive single varieties include 'Cinnebar', 30cm/12in high, which has burgundy-red flowers with yellow centres. The 25cm/10in high 'Naughty Marietta' has gold flowers with dark centres, while 'Sunny' is 30cm/12in high, with golden yellow, frilly flowers and 'Burgundy Ripple' is 30cm/12in high with rich, gold-edged orange-red flowers.

Double varieties of French marigold include the early-flowering 'Holiday Crested Mixed', 30cm/12in high, with large, uniform flowers, perfect for bedding or edging. 'Tiger Eyes', 30-35cm/12-14in high, has scarlet and dark orange chrysanthemum-like blooms, while 'Honeycomb', 25cm/10in high, has densely packed russet petals, edged in gold.

For window boxes, the 15cm/6in high 'Boy O' Boy' has bright orange flowers on compact plants. Unusually tolerant of wet or dry weather is 'Spanish Brocade', 20cm/8in high, with golden-edged, dark orange blooms. And for fully double, scarlet, camellia-like flowers, choose 'Scarlet Sophie', 25-30cm/10-12in high.

For a carpet effect grow 'Teeny Weeny'. Only 12cm/5in high, it forms a low-spreading mass of foliage, with single red and yellow blooms.

Afro-French marigolds

Sometimes called mule marigolds because they are sterile and do not set seed, Afro-French marigolds are F1 Triploid hybrids. Most are 25-40cm/10-16in high, and 30cm/12in across. They combine the shorter, bushier habit of French marigolds with the enormous, double blooms of African marigolds.

Good varieties include the bright-yellow 'Showboat', the

PERFECT PARTNERS

- In an informal setting, a dwarf conifer adds a focal point to a colour-themed planting of yellow marigolds, white alyssum and silver leafed senecio.
- For a circular island bed, plant an outer ring of yellow French marigolds, with taller, orange African marigolds on the inside, and canna in the centre, to provide height.
- In a hanging basket, combine French marigolds with nasturtiums. Nasturtiums come in the same colour range as the marigolds, and have masses of attractive, disc-shaped leaves which are ideal for hiding the potting compost as they trail, creating a curtain of greenery.

mahogany-tinged gold 'Seven Star Red' and the mixed 'Red and Gold Hybrids', up to 60cm/2ft high. 'First Lady' has clear yellow flowers, while 'Pineapple Crush', a dwarf form, 20cm/8in high, has buttercup-yellow blooms and the similar-sized 'Pumpkin Crush' has rich orange blooms.

Plants and seeds

When buying trays or pots of young plants, choose leafy, compact plants with plenty of

RINGING THE CHANGES

The signet or striped marigold (*T. tenuifolia pumila*) is an unusual relative of French and African marigolds. Its delicate-looking, small, single, starry flowers are produced in great quantities. The sweetly scented, ferny, light green leaves form a dome-shaped bush, ideal for edging, containers and massing informally in borders, spaced 15cm/6in apart.

The variety 'Tangerine Gem', 20cm/8in high, has large, deep-orange blooms. 'Paprika', 15cm/6in high, has copper-brown blooms, edged in gold; and 'Lulu', 20cm/8in high, has rich, canary-yellow flowers. 'Starfire', 15-20cm/6-8in high, comes in solid-coloured and two-toned blooms.

GARDEN NOTES

You can create different colour schemes with your marigolds, depending on the plants you choose to grow with them. This Tagetes tenuifolia 'Lemon Gem' looks 'warm' when it is growing next to the rich red and purple fuchsia, but much 'cooler' when it is combined with white alyssum.

Dwarf marigolds like these Tagetes tenuifolia (above) are useful for softening the edge of a path or lawn, but do not let this blind you to the glories of the taller varieties when viewed en masse, like this Tagetes tenuifolia 'Paprika Mixed' (below).

GO ORGANIC!

MARIGOLD WARFARE

African and French marigolds are traditional 'companion' plants, planted in rows in the vegetable garden. The strong scent of their leaves deters harmful insects from attacking crops. The roots of some species actually excrete a substance that can deter or even kill some soil pests.

WHAT WENT WRONG?

UNSUCCESSFUL SEEDS

Q Last spring I bought a pack of Afro-French marigold seeds and followed the instructions carefully, but only twelve plants ever came up. What did I do wrong?

A Probably nothing. Although they are fabulous plants, their one drawback is a lower than average germination rate. This year, buy two packs, and you should end up with plenty for a good display. Remember, too, that Triploid hybrid seed packs often contain fewer seeds than other types – check the packet before you buy.

flower buds. Avoid over-crowded plants and any with yellow leaves. Those in full flower may be tempting, but you will get a longer display if you stick to healthy plants in bud, with some colour showing, and maybe just one or two open blooms.

If you are buying seed packets, check the sell-by date. F1 hybrids have the largest, most uniformly sized and shaped flowers, especially important for formal bedding. They are more expensive than non-F1 hybrids, but you will find the difference in results well worth the extra initial cost.

Colour and form

Solid-colour African and French marigolds tend to have more impact from a distance than multi-coloured varieties, especially if the colour pattern is lacy or complex. Bright colours, such as lemon yellow or sharp orange, stand out well, especially against dark foliage. If, on the other hand, you want a rich, subtle effect, go for darker tones, or multi-coloured varieties featuring dark tones.

For an informal or wild garden, small, single flowers on spreading, bushy plants are

best, since they can mingle to form a solid mass. For a formal scheme, on the other hand, double flowers and narrow, upright plants are ideal.

If you want a riot of colour, some varieties are so prolific that the flowers completely hide the foliage, but for a more natural look, choose one with a high proportion of foliage to the number of flowers.

Display ideas

All French and African marigolds are ideal for container growing, since they have small root systems. Dwarf forms especially make first-class window box plants.

You can plant French and African marigolds in straight lines or blocks, or use them to edge a flower bed or path. Planted in groups of odd numbers, such as three, five, seven or nine, they can be used to create irregularly shaped clumps of colour.

Indoors, African and French marigolds are excellent as cut flowers, and both the whole flowers and the petals can be dried for flower arrangements, pressed flower pictures or for adding colour to pot pourri.

Honeysuckle

Sweet honeysuckle instantly evokes images of a country hedgerow. So easy to grow, this delightful shrub will fill your garden with its heady scent all summer.

Surely every cottage garden has a honeysuckle (lonicera), spreading a fragrant scent and attracting bees? If you want to bring a breath of country air into your garden, there couldn't be a simpler way than to plant a shrub or climbing honeysuckle. This beautiful plant is easy to grow

and the vigorous forms will give an attractive show even in their first year.

Most varieties are hardy, and happy in any well-drained soil. All honeysuckles are perennial, so they will give you pleasure year after year. There are many varieties of honeysuckle from which to

choose and a whole host of exciting things that can be done with them.

Shrubs and climbers

Some varieties are energetic climbers and may be used to camouflage or soften the lines of sheds, garages and fences. They can be trained to frame

This hybrid honeysuckle, L. × americana (above) will grow vigorously to cloak a wall or fence with its fragrant flowers and glossy foliage. To control it, either prune after flowering or cut off the old stems in winter.

The flowers of L × americana (left), a pretty combination of pink and yellow, stand out well against their background of dark green leaves and their heady fragrance will fill the garden all summer long.

PLANT PROFILE

Deciduous, semi-evergreen or evergreen shrubs and climbers with pretty, often very fragrant flowers. The perfect choice for clothing ugly walls, they will grow energetically providing camouflage in a year or two.

Suitable site and soil: sun or light shade in any well-drained, fertile soil, Add well-rotted manure, compost or bone meal at planting time and water in well. Add some sand if your soil tends to retain water.

Cultivation and care: prune climbers after flowering with shears, taking out any rampant, unruly trailers. Prune shrub varieties only to remove dead wood or hold back growth. Feed annually in winter or early spring.

Propagation: root semi-ripe cuttings (when the tip of the stem is still soft and green) towards the end of summer when growth is still strong. Alternatively, take hardwood cuttings (when the stem is hard and woody) in autumn. Stems that run along the ground will multiply naturally by 'layering'.

Pests and diseases: can be prone to aphids.

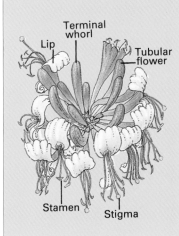

Terminal whorl

Lip

Tubular flower

Stamen

Stigma

This Japanese honeysuckle, L. japonica 'Halliana' (above) is a very vigorous climber, while L. periclymenum 'Belgica' (right), a variety of the common European honeysuckle or woodbine, can actually be quite invasive. Choose L. × brownii (below) with its brilliant red trumpets if you want a really bright splash of colour.

your front door or to cover an arch or pergola and will happily grow up walls as long as they are given some support.

Other varieties come in shrub form and can be used to brighten dull spots in your garden. One variety, *Lonicera nitida* can be trained to make a hedge that is an attactive change from privet.

Some shrubs and climbing varieties are evergreen, giving you foliage in the winter months. Others are deciduous.

The best place to grow
Your first tasks are to decide whether you want a climber or a shrub and to choose where

soil retains water, dig some sand into your site before planting. This will help moisture to drain through and prevent waterlogging.

Some popular climbers

L. americana is a good buy. The flowers are rose-purple in bud, turning creamy white as they open. It grows extremely rapidly, and can reach 9m/30ft if allowed to grow up and over a trellis. It is happiest adorning a west or east-facing wall.

L. periclymenum is also known as the woodbine or Dutch honeysuckle. There are two types from which to choose: early and late. The early variety, 'Belgica', blooms in early summer and then again at summer's end, while 'Serotina' flowers for just one period in early autumn.

These two varieties are such fast growers and are so hardy that many experts think they are the best of the climbers to buy. The woodbine can often be seen growing wild, and it is more resistant to pests and diseases than the more highly bred forms.

Both the early and the late flowering woodbine grow to

Box honeysuckle, L. nitida, grows vigorously to form a dense evergreen bush that will tolerate wind and salt spray. The variety 'Baggesen's Gold' has yellowy-green foliage. Left to form a natural shaped bush (above), it will brighten up even a shady corner of your garden. Grown as a hedge, it can be clipped to form a neat border on either side of a path or steps.

you want to put it. It is important to choose the variety which best fulfils your requirements, and suits the situation you have chosen.

The site will need very little preparation and the planning procedure is the same as for many shrubs and climbers. Add well-rotted manure or compost and some bone meal to the bottom of the hole and place your honeysuckle in position, gently teasing out its roots. Replace the soil and firm it down around your plant, then water well.

Although honeysuckles are not too fussy, they do appreciate good drainage. If your

HEALTHY AND HAPPY

To keep your plant healthy, there is no need to use pesticides and other chemicals, providing you follow certain golden rules.
● Buy the healthiest looking specimen you can find, checking the leaves and roots carefully.
● Cut down possible slug and snail damage by making sure you get rid of garden debris – pests quickly set up home in discarded plant pots.
● Be vigilant: at the first sign of aphids, spray with soapy water.
● Keep checking your plant: at the first sign of disease, prune out diseased parts and burn them.

GO ORGANIC!

30

away from full sun.

L. japonica 'Aureo-reticulata' is a variegated, evergreen climber whose leaves are mottled with gold. The flowers are scented and appear in summer months. It is hardy and will enjoy a sunny or semi-sunny aspect.

Other climbers have distinctive features. *L. henryi* is an evergreen that grows to about 4.5m/15ft and has small flowers followed by glossy

about 4.5m/15ft and this makes them ideal for growing over arches and pergolas as well as up walls and fences. The flowers appear in large clusters and are beautifully scented. They range from creamy white to vibrant yellow with pink or crimson buds and tubes.

It is a good idea to plant both varieties together in order to extend the flowering time. Both enjoy partial shade and are ideally placed facing

Chinese woodbine, L. tragophylla (above), has very large, showy flowers. All climbing honeysuckles have pretty, fragrant flowers such as these creamy 'Early Dutch' blossoms (right), while some varieties also have particularly attractive foliage, especially the yellow-veined leaves of L. japonica 'Aureo-reticulata' (below).

black berries *L. × brownii* is a semi-evergreen which is less vigorous than *L. × americana* and rather delicate. Its blooms are beautiful orange-scarlet.

Some popular shrubs
L. nitida is the type to use for hedging. It is evergreen, with small, neat leaves and creamy-white flowers. During the first two years of growth you will need to clip the hedge often to ensure that it forms a good bushy shape. After that, routine clipping as necessary is all that is required.

'Baggesen's Gold', a variety of *L. nitida*, is a slow growing shrub with decorative, golden leaves. The flowers are yellowish-green and are insignificant next to the foliage. It is just the plant to put in a corner that needs something striking to brighten it up. *L. syringantha* is a deciduous shrub with pale lilac flowers and a very strong scent.

Pruning and feeding
Prune honeysuckle by cutting away flowering shoots after flowering has finished.

31

Remove dead shoots if and when they appear. If the plant shows signs of getting unruly, cut away any shoots or tendrils that are making a nuisance of themselves. This may be done at any time, though after flowering is generally best. There are no special skills needed for pruning honeysuckle, so just snip away!

Feeding it up

Feed your honeysuckle every year by giving it a top dressing of well-rotted manure, or garden compost and a handful of bone meal. Add water at this stage so that the food finds its way through the soil to the roots more quickly.

This may be done at the beginning of winter or in very early spring. (Follow the maker's instructions when using any fertilizer, organic or chemical.)

For a stunning floral display combine complimentary climbers and grow clematis and honeysuckle together. Both are vigorous climbers and are very easy to grow. Pretty pink C. 'Ville de Lyon' (above) has flower centres that echo the colour and texture of the honeysuckle blossoms, while *C.* 'Lasurstern' (below) provides a brilliant colour contrast to honeysuckle, *L.x tellmanniana*.

Pelargoniums

A bright summer display of pelargoniums – often known as geraniums – will give your garden the Mediterranean touch.

Pelargoniums provide non-stop colour in sunny beds and borders as well as in containers, window boxes and hanging baskets. They provide bright flowers over a long period as well as attractively marked leaves to suit your seasonal colour schemes. Use them to create decorative features in every part of your garden this summer.

Pelargoniums come from hot, sunny climates, so give them the warmest position to make sure they thrive – though they will tolerate a little shade. They are tender and, if you wish to keep them growing from year to year, you will need to bring them indoors (or into a greenhouse) during the winter.

Planting out

Start your plants off on their annual growing season indoors and, once the danger of frost is past, set them out into their flowering positions in sunny borders or garden containers. You can also grow pelargoniums from seed or from small plantlets sold by nurseries or specialised outlets.

The flowers, usually carried in quite densely packed mop-head clusters, have five petals in the single varieties, and more in the double. Colours range from hot reds and oranges, through to deep burgundy and pale pinks. There are also white varieties. The soft leaves are sometimes

Pelargoniums are perfect container plants. In this stone 'geranium pot' (right) red and pink flowers cascade to great effect.

Pelargonium 'Apple Blossom' (above) is a zonal variety with particularly attractive double pink and white flowers. Other similar recommended varieties include 'Layton White' with its white single flowers and 'Penny', which has pretty pink double flowers.

Regal pelargoniums (below) are showy hybrids best on their own in pots so their colour and shape can be fully appreciated. There are a number of very beautiful varieties, including 'Grand Slam' with its bright red flowers and 'Autumn Festival' which has pink flowers with white throats.

attractively marked or coloured. You can use these showy plants in blocks of a single colour, but by choosing more subtle colours and combining them with other harmonious plants, you can create an integrated and stylish effect.

Pelargoniums come in an amazing array of shapes and sizes. The four most popular groups that you will enjoy using in the garden are zonal, regal, ivy-leaved trailing and scented-leaf types.

Popular pelargoniums

Zonal pelargoniums (*P.* × *hortorum*) offer a great variety of flower shapes and leaf colouring. There are single and double-flowered forms as well as some with spidery, cactus-like flowers and others with tightly rolled 'rosebud' flowers. The most common leaf colour is green, but the leaves usually

have a horseshoe-shaped zone or dark line breaking up the solid green colour.

Golden to amber leaves, two-colour variegation (usually green and cream) and tri-coloured leaves are also possible. All these variations add to the overall versatility of pelargoniums. There are also miniature and dwarf forms.

Regal pelargoniums (*P.* × *domesticum*) are hybrids bred from several different species and, although they are often used as houseplants, they can also be used in outdoor containers in the summer. They have large flowers (up to 5cm/ 2in wide), stiff stems and shrubby growth. They have a well-branched shape and grow to 45-60cm/18-24in high. Their leaves are serrated at the edges and slightly furled. Each flower has five to nine petals, and each head has about five bell-shaped flowers. The pet-

'Inca' (above right), a regal pelargonium with lovely deep red upper petals and pale pink lower petals is ideal for planting in a tub or trough to brighten up your patio or lawn. Choose a sunny or semi-shaded spot.

'Mrs Burdett Coutts' (right) is a lovely variety of zonal pelargonium. As well as its delightful clusters of bright red flowers, it has very attractive green leaves with reddish centres and a pretty edging of cream.

PLANT PROFILE

Suitable site and soil: sun is an important factor, but equally important are good drainage and a well-prepared, open site. Pelargoniums do not need very rich soils, but if the site has been used for spring bedding and much of its nutrients used up, dig it over well and add a balanced fertilizer when planting.

Cultivation and care: pelargoniums do not do well in waterlogged soils, so take care not to overwater them and make sure the drainage is good. In containers they need regular watering, especially during periods of drought. They can stand dry conditions, but should not be allowed to dry out completely. When you water them, direct the water onto the soil: try to avoid wetting petals and leaves if it is sunny as the sun will scorch them. Remove damaged and spent flowers regularly.

Propagation: take cuttings in summer to increase your stock, and pot up plants to overwinter indoors.

Many pelargoniums can be raised from hybrid seed sold by seed merchants. Look them up in a seed catalogue, but remember they may be found under 'geranium'.

Pests and diseases

Generally pelargoniums are easy to grow and trouble free. Whitefly and aphids can damage plants and spread infection, however. They coat stems and growing tips with waste sugars and this encourages infection such as black mould. If you use an insecticide, spray evenly and follow the manufacturer's instructions carefully.

Black mould is harmless but makes the plants look unsightly. It is difficult to remove but persistent rain will eventually wash it off.

Pelargonium rust creates yellow spots on the upper surface of leaves and raised, rusty circles on the lower side. Spray with a suitable fungicide at ten-day intervals. Check new plants for tell-tale signs.

Stem rot, wilt disease and viruses also affect pelargoniums. Burn or throw away the affected plants.

COLOUR COUNTS

For the best effect in borders plant zonal pelargoniums in threes or fives to get a block of colour. Use one colour so that you get a strong colour focus. If you are using fancy-leaved zonals apply the same principle. If you mix too many colours together, the result is likely to be rather muddled.

Pelargonium radula (below) has very pretty, delicate flowers with slim, veined petals. Its main interest, however, is in its leaves which have a delicious rose-lemon scent when touched. Plant this species next to a path where it will be brushed as you walk past, in a window box or patio pot, or anywhere that its fragrance can be enjoyed to the full.

Pelargonium graveolens (below) is another scented-leaved variety, this time smelling of lemons. It also has the bonus of rose-pink flowers with an unusual dark purple spot on the upper petals. Look out also for another unusual scented variety, P. tomentosum, which smells of peppermint.

als are wavy or ruffled and may be edged in a different colour to the main flower or streaked with darker colours. The colour range includes pink, purple, white and red. They can flower from spring through to late summer, but generally their flowering season is much shorter than that of the zonal pelargoniums and is confined to late spring and early summer.

Ivy-leaved pelargoniums (*P. peltatum*) offer a wide range of colour in single or double flowers, but their most attrac-

If you have a corner of the garden needing an instant injection of colour to brighten it up, simply use a pot of pelargoniums (above). Keeping the plants in pots means that, not only can you move them around wherever you wish, but as soon as there is a threat of frost, you can bring them indoors. Using several pots of pelargoniums to line the edge of a flight of steps (above right) gives a wonderfully sunny, Mediterranean effect, against the variegated greenery.

tive characteristic is their ivy-shaped leaves and trailing form. They are ideal for window boxes and hanging baskets. The leaves are often waxy and shiny, and some have dark markings.

Scented-leaf pelargoniums are a group of deliciously aromatic plants containing a number of species and their hybrids. The flowers are usually fairly small and often overlooked. They are pale in colour and, although pretty, it is the leaves that are the main attraction. Their strong scent

is released by even a gentle touch. Scented pelargoniums can smell of roses, lemons, nutmeg, apple and many other fragrances. Some have leaves that are variegated, some are deeply indented and some have dark markings.

They are suited to indoor cultivation all year round and in spring and summer they can be planted out to make a perfumed contribution to a herb garden, or placed in containers near the house.

Growing places

Zonal pelargoniums have long been traditional summer bedding plants. In combination with white alyssum and blue lobelia, red zonals have traditionally been used to make a summer splash for parks and public gardens. In your own less public bedding scheme you could use fancy-leaved 'Miss Burdett Coutts', a very old cultivated variety with small red flowers and cream, green and reddish leaves, as the feature plant. Combine it with a plain green-leaved zonal for an attractive contrast.

Regals are more tender and are often grown indoors as showpiece plants. If you want to grow them outdoors they will do well in containers on

The scarlet flowers of this potted pelargonium (right) look stunning against a brick wall. Try pelargoniums on patios or hanging in baskets next to the front door where they add a real touch of colour and style.

sunny patios or balconies.

Ivy-leaved pelargoniums are delightful plants for growing in containers: their tumbling, trailing growth pattern suits hanging baskets and window boxes, stone urns, terracotta pots and wall pots. Give them plenty of sunshine and combine them with your favourite summer plants, including other trailing foliage plants like ground ivy, ballota and ivy. Petunias, the blue Swan River daisy, pansies, nasturtiums are possible partners.

Graceful and formal stone urns are ideal for growing ivy-leaved pelargoniums. Set a well-shaped feature plant from your pelargonium in the centre and then underplant with your chosen variety of pelargoniums. They will then cascade over the edges, making a good display all through the summer.

Similarly, in window boxes, pelargoniums make a full and bold display.

PERFECT PARTNERS

Pelargoniums are good mixers. In this window box they are partnered with white petunias and the trailing effect of both plants softens the straight lines of the window frame.

Peonies

With their larger-than-life blooms, peonies are among the most popular herbaceous perennials. Luckily, they are as easy to grow and as long lived as they are gorgeous.

The much-loved peony vies with the rose for the title 'Queen of the Garden' in late spring and early summer. With their huge yet delicate-looking blooms in dazzling white, spun-sugar pastels and rich, deep hues, they have an old-fashioned, romantic appeal. Traditional mainstays in informal, country-cottage gardens and formal herbaceous borders, peonies are just as happy in the mixed beds and patio tubs of today's smaller gardens.

Peonies grow 45-90cm/1½-3ft high, with single, semi-double or double bowl-shaped flowers, up to 15cm/6in across and often fragrant. Colours range from white through cream, yellow, pink, lilac, scarlet and crimson to deep wine red. Some are two-toned, and many single varieties have showy yellow centres, or stamens.

The young spring shoots are delicately tinged with red and, unlike many other herbaceous perennials, whose leaves get tatty after flowering, the peony's glossy, deeply cut leaves remain attractive all summer long, providing a backdrop for other flowers. The leaves often take on rich, ruddy tones in autumn. Peonies also have exotic-looking, scarlet seed pods filled with shiny, midnight blue seeds to add interest in the garden or dried flower displays.

Peonies' fleshy, tuberous roots can take a year or two to settle down and start flower-ing after planting, but once they do, they virtually look after themselves, gradually forming sizeable clumps and producing generous crops of their beautiful satiny flowers for up to 50 years! Peonies are tolerant of intense heat and cold, too, and take severe winters and even the hottest summers in their stride.

Buying and planting

Buy container-grown plants, in early to mid-autumn or spring. Peonies like a deep

WHAT'S IN A NAME?

Peony was named after Paeon, physician to the Gods in Greek mythology, and has long been valued for its medicinal properties. Its seeds were worn to repel evil spirits; steeped in wine, to cure nightmares; and taken to ease childbirth pains. Peony roots, dried and ground and taken orally, were used to treat nervous disorders, including epilepsy. Don't however, attempt to treat yourself with peonies – see a doctor first!

root run, so dig a hole generously wider and deeper than the container. Remove all weeds, fork over the bottom and work in well-rotted garden compost, manure or bagged organic compost from garden centres.

Remove the plant from its pot. Plant with the crown 2.5cm/1in below ground level, replace the soil, mixed with more organic matter, and firm. Sprinkle a handful of bone meal over the soil, and water if the soil is dry. If planting more than one, space them 60-90cm/ 2-3ft apart, according to type.

Using peonies

Depending on height, peonies can go in the front, middle or back of a bed or border. Their clumpy foliage is ideal for hiding bare or awkward-looking stems, such as those of hybrid tea or floribunda roses. They are also most attractive when planted as an infill between

The combination of glossy, lance-shaped leaves and nodding crimson double flowers makes a dramatic splash in a mixed spring border (above), where it is set off by the golden-green bracts of Euphorbia.

There are hundreds of varieties of Chinese peony (P. lactiflora). 'Sarah Bernhardt' (left) is a particularly attractive double, with large, scented flowers.

Often classified as semi-doubles, anemone-form peonies have a double row of outer petals and a centre that fills as the flower matures with modified stamens. In 'Bowl of Beauty' (right), these petaloids make a delicious, creamy contrast to the pink petals.

WATCH POINTS

- When hoeing the ground near peonies, be careful not to pierce or nick the fleshy crowns; they are liable to rot. It is also best not to fork the ground very near peonies.
- If couch grass, bindweed or ground elder gets into peony crowns, it is a real nightmare, so check regularly and remove any weeds while they are still small.
- When applying a mulch, spread it around, not over, the peony crown, or it may fail to flower properly.

shrubs in a mixed border.

A long, narrow border of one peony variety edging a path or wall is stunning in flower.

For a wild garden, single varieties look most natural, and for an authentic cottage garden look, use one of the old-fashioned favourites such as double crimson *P. officinalis* 'Rubra Plena'.

For container growing, choose a compact type, such as the fern-leafed peony, 45cm/18in high and wide.

Tree peonies

In spite of their name, tree peonies grow no more than 1.2-1.8m/4-6ft high and wide, and form picturesque, multi-stemmed, wide-spreading shrubs. These unusual and striking plants are a little more challenging to grow, but a tree peony in full flower is a sight you won't forget!

Like herbaceous peonies, tree peonies are long lived,

The single-flowered species P. arietina *(above) is very similar to* P. mascula. *The main distinguishing feature is that the underside of* arietina's *leaves are covered in fine hairs.*

P. lactiflora *'Nancy Lindsay' (right) can be hard to find. It is well worth tracking down, however, for its pale apricot flowers containing a nest of golden yellow stamens.*

CLOSED BUDS

Q Why do my peonies look healthy, but the buds stay hard and small, and never open?

A It could be a number of things; dry soil, lack of food, being planted too deeply, disturbed roots or frost damage. By process of elimination, you should be able to sort this out, and correct it.

RECOMMENDED VARIETIES

- *Paeonia anomala* has finely cut leaves and crimson red, single flowers with yellow stamens in late spring.
- *P. arietina* has pink, single flowers with creamy yellow stamens in late spring.
- *P. lactiflora*, or Chinese peony, includes literally hundreds of varieties, often scented, with a huge range of colour and form. Flowers appear in early summer.

  Among the most popular are the single flowered 'White Wings' and crimson 'Lord Kitchener'. Semi-double varieties include the pale pink and cream 'Bowl of Beauty' and the rosy pink, yellow-centred 'Globe of Light'. Full doubles include the apple blossom pink 'Sarah Bernhardt', the ruby red 'Felix Supreme', creamy white 'Bowl of Cream', and the blush pink 'Moonstone'.
- *P. mlokosewitschii*, commonly called 'Molly the Witch' because of its almost unpronounceable real name, has greeny grey, downy leaves and single yellow flowers with golden stamens which appear in mid-spring.
- *P. tenuifolia*, the fern-leaved peony, has delicate ferny foliage and single, deep crimson, shiny flowers with golden stamens. 'Plena' has double crimson flowers; 'Rosea' has pink flowers.

The leaves of P. tenuifolia (top) are deeply divided into long, thin segments, making a finely-textured backdrop for a single crimson flowers with their contrasting yellow anthers.

PERFECT PARTNERS

- Peonies, lupins, bearded iris, delphiniums and campanulas are the backbone of a traditional early summer border.
- For a handsome trio, combine double pink peonies with rich blue delphiniums behind and lady's mantle (Alchemilla) in front.
- For an all-pink theme with old-fashioned charm, plant pink roses, hardy geraniums, sweet Williams and peonies.
- Orange wallflowers, yellow species roses, yellow tulips and the yellow 'Molly the Witch' peony (P. mlokosewitschii) make a bright, sunny late spring display.

- Plant hyacinth among Chinese peonies, whose shoots are rosy red when the hyacinths flower. When the hyacinths finish, the peonies come into their own.
- The tall pink and mauve flower spikes of foxgloves (Digitalis purpurea) make a pleasing backdrop for pink double peonies (right).
- Plant a late-flowering clematis to ramble through a clump of peonies, adding interest after the peonies finish. C. flammula, with scented white flowers, or the orange peel clematis, C. orientalis, with thick-petalled, yellowy orange bell flowers, are just two possibilities.

The single flowered P. mlokosewitschii, 'Molly the Witch' (above) is an old garden favourite, and is much valued for its large lemon-yellow flowers and soft, faintly bluish foliage.

with deeply divided, deciduous leaves and large, showy flowers in late spring and early summer. The flowers come in single, semi-double and double forms, and whites, pinks, yellows and reds, some with contrasting blotches.

Tree peonies make lovely focal points in mixed borders and woodland gardens, but are also impressive enough to be used as specimen plants on a lawn. For an exquisite garden 'painting', underplant a tree peony with violets.

Growing tree peonies

Tree peonies are very hardy, but young growth is easily damaged by spring frost, especially after a mild winter. Fertile, moist but well drained soil in sun or light shade is best; shelter from the wind and late frosts is essential .

Container-grown tree peonies should be planted in early to mid-spring. Plant them deeply, with any graft, or join, between the named variety and rootstock 10cm/4in below

Some peony varieties have flowers so large that they flop over unless each bloom is individually supported. This need not be a disaster (above); the delicate pink of the double lactiflora shows well against the grey of the gravel path.

PICK A PEONY

Among the most popular cut flowers and superb focal points for flower arrangements, peonies are long lasting if you pick them in bud, but with colour showing. Lay them down flat on a cool floor overnight, then re-cut the stem ends and place in a deep container of warm water for several hours before arranging. Only take one or two flowers per plant.

Pick the seed pods while still green, and hang them upside down to dry. You can preserve the leaves of tree peonies by picking them when mature but still green, and placing them in a tall container of half glycerine, half warm water. Leave them until they turn leathery and grey green, topping up the liquid if necessary.

BRIGHT IDEAS

P. × smouthii (right) is an old lactiflora variety that came to Britain from France in 1845. Now rarely seen, it was once highly valued for its lacy leaves and crimson, single flowers, which appear earlier than most peony varieties.

P. lutea ludlowii (right) is a tree peony which grows to a height and spread of 2.4m/8ft. Attractive though its fragrant, cup-shaded single yellow flowers are, it is more often planted for its show of vivid green, deeply divided leaves.

The flowers of the tree peony P. suffruticosa have a splash of colour at the base of each petal. 'Rock's Variety', also known as 'Joseph Rock' (above), has white petals and a maroon blotch. Other varieties are pink, with chocolate-brown splashes.

the soil surface. Scatter bone meal on top.

You can grow species tree peonies from seed, but they take several years to flower. Varieties are usually propagated by grafting, a technique best left to experts, but if you have a variety growing on its own roots, you can divide it in early autumn.

Once established, tree peonies need to be mulched, fed and dead-headed in the same way as herbaceous varieties. Otherwise the only maintenance necessary is to cut back any damaged or dead wood in the spring.

Peony wilt also affects tree peonies, especially those planted in damp or crowded conditions. Their roots may be susceptible to honey fungus; there is no cure, and affected plants should be destroyed.

Rhododendrons

Everyone can grow these beautiful, dazzling shrubs – the aristocrats of the plant world – either in the garden or in tubs and window boxes.

From the dense forests of the Himalayas, across Burma and Tibet into southwest China, intrepid plant hunters of the past have searched the mountains to discover many of the beautiful rhododendron species that people enjoy today. One can also find the rhododendron family growing naturally across Alaska, through Canada and down the East and West coasts of North America.

In the wild there are over 500 different species of all sizes from tall 20m/65ft trees to ground-hugging alpines.

From the wide range of these beautiful shrubs found in nature, plant breeders have hybridized a vast choice of the most attractive flowering shrubs that can brighten your garden. There is a dazzling

Wherever rhododendrons are planted, in a small garden (above) or an area of natural woodland, they will produce a splash of dramatic colour in spring or summer. Several planted together will produce a bank of one colour or a variety of complementary hues.

RHODODENDRON OR AZALEA?

The plants that we call azaleas are really rhododendrons – you will find them listed under rhododendrons in some books and catalogues. They differ from rhododrendrons in that they are often deciduous (and those described as evergreen are not true evergreens because the leaves formed on the lower parts of the shoots fall in autumn). In this feature we have included only the true rhododendrons and not azaleas. The popular tender azalea sold as a pot plant in the winter is really *Rhododendron simsii.*

GARDEN NOTES

display of colours from pinks to white, creamy yellows, orange, scarlet, crimson and lavender. A number of rhododendrons also have an exquisite scent and others have highly aromatic foliage. Flowering seasons of the different types occur at various times of the year from winter through to summer.

In terms of size, the vast range of rhododendrons available from garden centres and nurseries ensures that everyone has an opportunity to enjoy these beautiful flowering shrubs. The smallest will adorn a window box, there are many suitable for tubs, and the largest will need a woodland site to spread themselves.

Nearly all rhododendrons are evergreen and belong to the ericaceous family, which includes azaleas and heathers. This whole family has one particular requirement – the soil must be acid. This means that no quantity of lime should be present. Planted into the wrong soil your rhododendron's leaves will look yellow and sad. But do not despair if you have alkaline soil. It is quite easy to grow rhododendrons in pots and tubs using

Growing a rhododendron in a large flowerpot (above) is a way of introducing colour to an otherwise drab corner of a patio. The variety above is 'Baden-Baden'.

The pure white flowers of the dwarf variety 'Ptarmigan' (below) contrast well with more colourful plants such as primulas.

PLANT PROFILE

Site and soil:
Rhododendrons require well drained soil, moist, acid and rich in humus. Avoid badly drained soil that stays wet in winter. Also, don't subject them to dry conditions. They need plenty of water during drought. Use rainwater if possible; mains water is often quite alkaline (chalky).

Alkaline soil is also no good for them. But if your garden soil is chalky, you can give your rhododendron its own special soil within a tub or other container, using ericaceous compost.

All rhododendrons are happy in light shade which guards them from late spring frosts and keeps the ground cool and moist. Few enjoy heavy shade but some dwarf alpines tolerate a sunny site or even a rockery.

Cultivation and care: Care at the planting stage almost guarantees success. First make sure the site and soil are right. Then make the hole suitably wide and shallow for the rootball, so that the final soil level comes to the base of the stem, not above!

Inside the hole, provide plenty of moss peat or, better, leaf mould or coconut fibre. Water in well, using rainwater if you can. Keep rhododendrons well watered during dry spells, or whenever their leaves hang.

The best soil conditioning is to add mulch each spring: at least 2.5cm/1in of humus (leaf mould etc.). Fertilizer is seldom necessary at all.

To ensure strong growth, remove old flowerheads a month or so after flowering. This makes sure that all the energy goes into growing and not into forming seeds.

Little pruning is necessary except where suckers on a hybrid grow from below a graft and these should be cut away. You will notice the different leaf form (usually it is *Rhododendron ponticum*) which characterizes the sucker growth.

Problems, pest and diseases:
Rhododendrons have few problems. If the leaves look pale, a spring application of sulphate of ammonia may help and will increase the soil acidity a little, but it may be necessary to use Sequestrene (see box).

Browning of the leaf tips indicates too much or too little water, and the growing conditions need to be adjusted accordingly.

Bark split can occur after a very cold spring. Shoots appear to die back beyond where bark has split away, and need to be pruned back to healthy wood.

Greenfly can attack the fresh shoots of young plants – this can be controlled with a pyrethrum-based spray.

Weevils cut tell-tale notches in the leaves. Although disfiguring, these will not kill the plants.

Propagation:
Rhododendrons are quite easy to propagate from cuttings or by layering. Grafting is sometimes used commercially but is difficult for an amateur, as you will need a suitable rootstock as well as a fair amount of skill.

They can be raised from seed, but this is a slow method and only suitable for the species – the large hybrids will not produce plants like the parent.

Take cuttings from semi-ripe shoots, choosing a healthy plant, preferably in late summer. The length of the cutting depends on the species: 5-8cm/2-3in for the tender *R. simsii*, about 15-23cm/6-9in for most hardy species.

Rooting is usually accelerated by dipping the end in a rooting hormone. Lightly wounding the base first may help. Insert the cuttings in pots in a mixture of equal parts moss peat and sharp sand (or perlite). They should root if kept in a cold frame, but they will probably root best if you can place them in a propagator.

Once they have rooted, pot each one in an ericaceous compost, and grow on until large enough to plant out. It may take up to five years before they flower.

Layering is a good way to produce one or two of your favourite plants. See PART 7, *Gardener's Diary* for instructions on how to layer a rhododendron.

RECOMMENDED VARIETIES

For very small gardens and rockeries

Blue Diamond	(blue)
Baden-Baden	(red)
Carmen	(deep scarlet)
Cilpinense	(pink)
Curlew	(yellow)
Dora Amateis	(white)
R. impeditum	(lavender)
Scarlet Wonder	(scarlet)
Ptarmigan	(white)
Patty Bee	(yellow)
Ginny Gee	(white and pink flush)

For pots and tubs

Percy Wiseman	(pink and cream)
Pink Cherub	(soft pink)
Golden Torch	(pale yellow)
Surrey Heath	(rose pink)
Titian Beauty	(geranium red)
Elizabeth	(scarlet)
Praecox	(lavender)

For hedges and screens

Britannia	(scarlet)
Cunningham's White	(white)
R. ponticum	(lavender)

For large woodland gardens

Autumn Gold	(apricot/ salmon)
Christmas Cheer	(pink; winter flowering)
Doncaster	(scarlet)
Elizabeth de Rothschild	(cream)
Gomer Waterer	(white flushed lavender)
Kluis Sensation	(scarlet)
Lord Roberts	(red)
Nova Zembla	(bright red)
Pink Pearl	(pink)
Purple Splendour	(deep purple)
Unique	pink fading to cream

an acid compost and watering with soft rainwater.

Since many rhododendrons originate from the high, often snow-covered hills of the Himalayas, they are fairly used to occasional cold winters and can generally be described as quite hardy. However, there are a few very early spring varieties and the beautiful flowers of these are sometimes damaged by the frost. Try to find a well sheltered site for such plants, perhaps tucked under the shade of a suitable tree or shrub to give protection from frost and cold dry winds.

If you have a cool greenhouse or conservatory from which you can exclude the frost, this will allow you to grow the most exquisite range of fragrant rhododendrons.

CURING A SICKLY PLANT

Rhododendrons growing on soil that is not sufficiently acid for their liking often grow poorly and the leaves may look pale and yellow. You can often help the plant survive by feeding it with Sequestrene, which contains iron and other elements in a form that the plant can absorb even though it is not growing in an acid soil.

GROWING TIPS

Rhododendron 'Blue Diamond' (above) is one that likes full sun. It grows to a height of 1.5m/5ft and flowers from mid- to late spring.

Gardeners with space will want to contrast several varieties (above right). They can be underplanted with flowering and foliage plants. Here foxgloves, ferns, lady's mantle and Epimedium have been used.

The correct choice of varieties planted next to each other can give a succession of flowers over a sustained period. 'Christmas Cheer' (left) is in flower in late winter, ahead of other species.

The large but compact cherry-red flowers of 'Britannia' (right) appear in late spring and early summer.

These give you wonderful colour and scent during the first days of early spring. Like all your rhododendrons, the greenhouse ones require exactly the same acid, lime-free compost. After flowering they can be plunged, with their pots, into the garden, provided you are sure the soil is not alkaline. However, remember to bring them back indoors before the first frost of autumn.

A wide choice

Across many regions of Britain the large *Rhododendron ponticum* has become naturalized in woods and on open moorlands, producing a mass of deep purple in late spring and early summer. This lovely plant was introduced into the country from Turkey about 200 years ago. Unfortunately, it has been almost too successful in spreading from seed, and foresters are liable to look upon it as quite a serious weed. However, in the garden it remains useful because it offers you a quick-growing plant that will form an excellent, hardy evergreen hedge or high screen that will flower profusely in late spring. Equally effective as hedges and screens are 'Cunningham's White' and the brilliant scarlet 'Britannia'.

Many smaller rhododendron species naturally occur at quite high altitudes on open mountain sides, some as high as 3,600m/12,000ft. These and their hybrids can be quite truthfully described as al-

'Purple Splendour' is one of the larger varieties, growing to 3m/10ft. The rich purple blooms have black speckles in the throat and creamy stamens.

GROWING TIPS

REPLANTING

Rhododendrons make shallow fibrous roots that form a tight root ball. With care quite large plants can be moved around the garden. Ideally do this in late autumn. Water the rhododendron well after replanting.

what everyone would like to achieve in the garden. However, because rhododendrons have a limited flowering season, careful thought must be given to suitable companion planting for them.

Suitable companions

Attractive trees which give rhododendrons the necessary frost protection and the light dappled shade which keeps the roots cool and moist, can add some colour of their own.

Flowering cherries contribute lovely pastel shades and the showy mespilus (*Amelanchier canadensis*), a most effective white. Many varieties of mountain ash (*Sorbus aucuparia*) look well among rhododendrons, and the lovely autumn tints of Japanese maples add a touch of brightness at the end of the year.

On the ground below the usual hybrid rhododendrons it is good to plant groups of heather or perhaps hostas, whose bold leaves may be striped green and white or pale yellow. One obvious sort of companion is the lovely azalea. This is a close relation of the rhododendron and requires the same conditions.

It says something about rhododendrons that over the past 100 years the rich and famous have fallen deeply in love with their exotic charm. Here we have what must surely be the aristocrats of the plant world, yet they provide a magnificent range of flowering evergreens that are now available for all to enjoy. With some care, it is possible for everyone to share their beauty.

pines. They offer us a wide selection of low-growing plants that will tolerate full sun and thrive in cool, moist conditions. All these dwarf plants can be put to great use in a small garden and can be equally effective in a rock garden or raised bed provided the soil is suitable.

Maximum interest and colour throughout the year is

PERFECT PARTNERS

Trees that grow well with rhododendrons are small *Acers* (Japanese maple); birch; flowering cherries (spring varieties); *Prunus autumnalis* (autumn flowering cherry); liquidambar; rowan (mountain ash); and *Malus* (flowering crab apple).

Shrubs that associate well with rhododendrons include azaleas, heathers, pernettyas, daphnes, viburnums, skimmias, dwarf berberis and pieris.

Pansies

**Pansies' velvety textures and friendly little faces
make them one of the best-loved garden flowers,
providing colour all year round.**

Perhaps the pansy's place in our affections comes from its long association with lovers. The word pansy comes from the French *pensées,* meaning 'thoughts'. The charming flowers both of pansies and of their close relatives, violas, were said to turn a person's thoughts to their loved one. Their old English name, heartsease, symbolized the peace and rest that came to the hearts of lovers who died of love.

Yet, in stark contrast to this romantically melancholy image of tormented sweethearts, the pansy itself is essentially a cheerful plant. Not only does it present a bright and breezy countenance to the world, but it is amenable and obliging by nature too.

Pansies are simple to grow from seed and will put up with almost any soil. They are also very easy to obtain as bedding plants. Garden centres always carry a thorough selection and

most little local stores such as greengrocers, florists and even pet shops often offer trays of pansies for sale.

There are a host of varieties available, in almost every colour. Most varieties have at least two contrasting shades. In some cases this is a fringe around the petals; others have 'faces' of another colour at their centres.

If you browse through catalogues or the seed racks at your local garden centre, you

The rich and varied colours of pansies (above) allow you to create an air of profusion in a small space and for little cost or effort. Some of the tones are unique and magical and, with care and a little luck, you can produce fine blooms throughout the year.

will discover varieties of pansies for every season and, with care and a mild winter, you could have a colourful display all year round.

Winter pansies

Winter can be a very dull time in your garden. This is especially true if your space is limited to a small patch, a balcony or a window box or two. There is simply no room for the shrubs, trees and heathers that provide most of the winter interest in larger gardens.

The ever-obliging pansy can brighten up the winter gloom. 'Winter Smiles' and 'Forerunner Mixed' are two colourful varieties which will flower from autumn through to early spring in mild winters.

The 'Universal' F1 hybrid varieties are also winter flowering and come in selections of

You can really let your creativity show when you put pansies in hanging baskets. This ball-like effect (right) has a simple colour scheme. Just think what you can do with a richer mix! Pansies are hardy plants so your hanging basket can endure harsh days.

'King of the Blacks' (below) are among the most mysterious of all garden pansies. They are robust plants with flowers nestling deep in the foliage. They reach a breadth of 10cm/4in or more.

PLANT PROFILE

Suitable site and soil: will tolerate most soils but benefit from some prior preparation. Dig well and add well-rotted manure and a dusting of bone meal to the top 23cm/9in.

Planting: in spring or autumn, about 20-30cm/8-12in apart in full sun or partial shade.

Propagation: from seed or cuttings. Sow seeds according to the instructions on the packet. May be sown indoors or out. Cuttings should be taken from fresh new growth in spring or autumn. Stop the parent plant from flowering in July by removing buds, encouraging the vigorous new growth you will need in autumn. Choose sturdy stems and cut just below a joint. Trim away lower leaves. Add horticultural sand and perlite to the compost and fill trays to 10cm/4in. Make holes and add a little sand to the bottom of each. Firm in 6-8cm/2½-3in

cuttings and water well. Place in a shady spot. Plant out spring cuttings in autumn but over-winter autumn cuttings in a sunny, unheated cold frame.

Pests and diseases: rarely troubled by common pests such as slugs, snails and aphids. Red spider mite can sometimes be controlled by directing a jet of water at the creatures and their webs until all trace is washed away. The rare, soil-borne *pansy sickness* can kill off healthy plants almost overnight. Discard infected plants and start again in another site, or replace the topsoil in the infected area. Sinking pansies in pots into the bed is another solution.

Recommended varieties: Any 'Universal' will give winter flowers. Try 'Padparadja' and 'Clear Crystals' for self-colour and, for fun, 'Jolly Joker', the dwarf 'Baby Lucia' or 'Rippling Waters'.

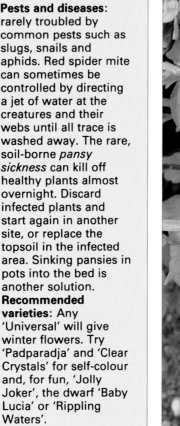

Looking like a butterfly, the 'Joker Light Blue' pansy (left) has sharp colours and commands attention anywhere. The Joker varieties are among the ever-growing number of novelty plants whose patterns can be blended endlessly.

'Padparadja' (below) is named after a real jewel of the Orient. This plant takes on even more luxurious tones when planted among other pansies. A summer pansy, it offers a garden a broad swathe of colour or a rich splash in a drab corner.

colours and types. The multi-coloured 'Delft', for example, has flowers that are lemon, cream, purple, white and midnight black, while 'Beaconsfield' is a beautiful royal purple shading to lilac, with light blue upper petals.

The unromantic sounding 'White Blotch' is a neat, compact plant, pure white with a deep violet blue face or 'blotch'. There is also a 'Blue Blotch', whose petals are a deep, rich blue tinged with purple. It has a distinctive velvet blue face.

If you prefer flowers in all one colour, without a face, the self-coloured varieties are for you. Amongst the winter flowerers there is 'True Blue', which is a clear mid-blue and has rather fetching whiskers. Other single-coloured varieties include a pure white and a wonderful apricot.

For smaller winter flowering plants choose 'Floral Dance', which will give you a lovely mixture of blooms. To ensure that there is no gap in flowering between the winter

and summer varieties, plant some earlies. 'Eclipse' is one such variety, beginning its flowering very early in the season and finishing at the end of the summer. Another possible choice is 'Supremo', which offers yellow, bronze, red, rose, purple and white in its colour combinations. It has very large flowers.

'Ruffled Earlies', as their name suggests, have ruffled edges and flower in early spring. To add to their charms, they may sometimes have contrasting borders, veins, stripes or blotches.

Summer blooms

Most pansies flower in summer and early autumn and there are many varieties to choose from in this category. Some of these can produce very large flowers, bi-coloured, tri-coloured or multi-coloured. 'Majestic Giant', 'Swiss Giant' and 'Monarch Giant' are all mixtures and will provide rich colours. Some of the blooms in these mixtures will have strongly marked faces.

For self-coloured pansies with a wide selection of colours, it is hard to beat the 'Clear Crystal Mixed' variety.

Fancies

Among the summer lovers there is a wide choice of what Victorian gardeners referred to as 'fancies'. These are strikingly-coloured novelty plants whose numbers are added to every year. 'Jolly Joker', for instance, is an orange and purple bi-colour with a fairly small flower. 'Rippling Waters'

CREATING VARIETIES

Pansies are very obliging and you can have a lot of fun developing your own new varieties. Simply set aside a small area devoted to a few favourites and allow nature to take its course. Allow the plants to set seed and see what happens next. Some plants produced this way will be truly gorgeous; others, unfortunately, may turn out to be more useful in the compost bin.

BRIGHT IDEAS

is a splendid dark purple bloom enhanced with rippled white edges.

'Joker' is pale blue with a dark blue face and a little white for contrast. 'Love Duet' is cream suffused with pale pink and has a rich rose face.

For intensity of colour and a stunning display you could not do better than to choose 'Padparadja', which is a really deep, rich orange variety. It glows like the Sri Lankan jewel after which it is named. If you enjoy a really dramatic effect, plant it with the equally exotic 'Midnight Black' or another variety of the same colour, 'Black Star'.

Choosing

Pansies offer such a wealth of possibilities in terms of colour, design and flowering season, that it is easy to get confused.

The first thing to decide is when you want them to flower. With care you can select varieties which will flower one after another so that every month of the year is graced by their presence in your garden.

The next consideration is where you want to plant them. Pansies are equally happy as border plants or container dwellers. They also make very effective edging plants.

Like most bedding plants, pansies enjoy full sun, but they will tolerate some shade.

This array of 'Monarch' pansies (left) have been orchestrated to resemble a painting. 'True Blue' pansies (below left) are a reminder that they can be subtly shaded as well as vibrantly coloured.

The aptly named 'Jolly Joker' (above) is among the most reliable pansies for summer blooms.

The exquisite 'Love Duet' (right) is one of the most striking of all pansy varieties.

PERFECT PARTNERS

Potted pansies look good when combined with slightly taller flowers. These blue violas and white tulips (above) make a dramatic effect.

Unlike their close relatives, violets and some violas, they are not suited to brightening a very shady corner.

Mix and match

Design is the next consideration. Many devotees of the pansy feel that they are at their resplendent best when masses of the same variety are planted together in a border or container. This is particularly true of self-coloured varieties.

However, pansies also make good companion plants. The more old-fashioned varieties, for example, make a handsome addition to a knot garden. Their old-world charm blends beautifully with the historical theme of this type of planting scheme. Box hedges and the foliage of selected herbs make a wonderful background for their jaunty, colourful blooms. Choose fairly tidy herbs such as chives, thyme, parsley and basil. Pansies cannot compete with unruly types such as mint.

Pansies look well with small bulbs such as snowdrops, *Iris reticulata*, cyclamen and muscari. Their bold colours and markings complement the more delicate features of miniature bulbs. The shapes go well together too.

Delphiniums

Picture an ideal cottage garden or a perfect herbaceous border; there, towering above it all, are the majestic blooms of the delphinium.

Delphiniums manage, somehow, to combine a regal charm with a cosy familiarity. They seem to be equally at ease in a humble cottage garden or in the formal borders of a stately home.

There are several good reasons why generations of gardeners have included delphiniums in their planting schemes. Hardy plants come in a whole host of reds, purples, pinks and yellows, but true blues are more difficult to find. Delphiniums offer a wide range of truly glorious blues, from the very pale to very dark, rich hues.

The stately shape of delphiniums adds to their appeal. They bring much needed height to the back of borders and to the centre of island beds, while their impressive flower spikes contrast well with the gentler outlines of other border plants.

Delphiniums are hardy plants, well able to survive almost any weather except drought and strong winds. Howling gales will play havoc with the very tall forms, so it pays to provide support early in the growing season by placing three 1.2m/4ft bamboo stakes in a triangle around each plant. Tie the stems in as necessary as the plants grow. Alternatively, commercial supports are available.

Dwarf delphiniums

Dwarf varieties have been developed primarily to combat the hazards of sites exposed to the winds. You lose very little in the way of flower spikes by choosing dwarf varieties, but the foliage is much more compact. In a very windy area it will still be necessary to provide some support.

Most delphiniums are perennial and are capable of giving pleasure for many years, though there are hardy annual species, the larkspurs, which are derived from *Delphinium ajacis* and *D. consolida*.

Blues plus

A wide range of colours is available, apart from the famous blues. There are dazzling whites, dusky pinks, subtle creams and rich purples as well. Recent developments include clear pinks, a salmon/orange and brilliant reds from the University Hybrid range of plants. With this selection to choose from it is possible to work delphiniums into any garden colour scheme.

Humble origins

The gorgeous hybrid delphiniums that we grow in our gardens today are the result of cross-breeding by keen amateurs, specialist growers and accidental pollination by enthusiastic bees.

The raw material for this work are close on a hundred species of wild delphinium that are to be found scattered throughout the world. Few of these wild plants are useful in the garden, as they are often insignificant to look at and difficult to grow. However, there are some species delphiniums available from specialists.

In some delphiniums, such as 'Gordon Forsyth' (below), the flower spikes are 1.8m/6ft tall. Others, like the larkspur, 'Dwarf Hyacinth Mixed' (below right), are just 30cm/1ft. All of them make a strong vertical line in an herbaceous border. Different heights and colours can be used in a mixed planting to great effect (right).

PLANT PROFILE

Suitable site and soil An open sunny site with fertile, well drained soil is best. Will tolerate any type of soil as long as it is well prepared.

Cultivation and care May be planted at any time between spring and autumn, but spring is best. They like a well-settled root run, so prepare the site in advance if possible. Must have plenty of water during spring. Apply a thick mulch of spent mushroom compost or garden compost in early spring to help retain moisture. Feed established plants with a top dressing of blood, fish and bone meal in winter or early spring.

Propagation Experts disagree on whether or not to split crowns to increase stock. Taking cuttings in early spring is the safest bet. Cut young shoots 5-10cm/2-4in long as near to the woody crown as possible. Discard hollow or discoloured shoots. Plant cuttings in damp silver sand or vermiculite and place in a shaded cold frame or greenhouse. They should root within 6-8 weeks. Pot on or plant out in a nursery bed and move to a permanent position early in the following spring.

Sow seeds thinly on the surface of moist seed compost. Cover with a thin layer of compost. Cover with a lid or foil and keep at a temperature of about 60°F(15°C). Some seeds will germinate within days, others may take months. When sufficiently grown, prick out and plant in individual 5cm/2in pots. Remember that plants do not always come true from seed.

Pests and diseases Very susceptible to slug damage during winter and early spring. Cover crowns with sharp sand or similar in winter. Clear dead leaves and other debris from around your plants. Caterpillars of the delphinium moth are best removed by hand if possible. Mildew can occur; spray with a fungicide at the first sign of trouble. Good cultivation discourages mildew. Waterlogged soil may cause crown-rot. There is no remedy for this. Root out the affected crowns and plant new stock. It is good general practice to take cuttings of your favourites, so that you can replace them if necessary.

It is possible to grow delphiniums from seed but the results are often disappointing. Hybrids are notorious for not growing true from seed and therefore you are best advised to buy plants from specialist growers. Reference to a plant finder should yield their names and addresses.

On receipt of their catalogues you will be astonished at the sheer number of named varieties available. Each nursery has a number of their very own, as well as the more usual types.

Where to plant

Delphiniums enjoy full sun and an open site. They should not have to compete for moisture with thirsty tree and shrub roots nearby. Their traditional home in a herbaceous border or an island bed is a practical and very effective choice of site.

If your garden is small, it is quite possible to grow delphiniums in large containers. You could manage to fit two or three dwarf varieties into a half barrel, for example. Plant a few trailing plants at the edges to soften the outline and a couple of pretty perennials and annuals to sustain interest after the delphiniums have ceased flowering.

The secret of success with delphiniums and herbaceous beds lies in choosing and preparing the site. The soil must

Although best known for the blue varieties, such as 'Lord Butler' (far right), there are many other colours in the delphinium's palette, including the pink of 'Langdon's Royal Flush' (right) and the pure white of 'Olive Poppleton' (below).

be very fertile for large-flowered varieties. Although delphiniums like plenty of water, especially in spring, drainage must be good.

Preparing the site

Try to think far enough ahead to prepare the site in the autumn before planting in early spring. Although it is possible to prepare the ground when you are doing the planting, it is best to allow time for the site to settle. Delphiniums like a firm root run.

Bearing in mind that delphiniums need to be well fed and watered, dig plenty of organic matter such as well-rotted manure or good garden compost into the bed. This will ensure that they get plenty of nutrients and, paradoxically, will supply good drainage while retaining moisture.

Dig in blood, fish and bone meal at a rate of roughly 100g/4oz per sq.m./sq.yd. This will supply nourishment that is released slowly and steadily over the growing period.

Planting out

Spring is the best time to plant delphiniums, but you may have to wait until the following year for blooms.

You can plant in the autumn, which will ensure some sort of show the following summer, though there is a risk that more vulnerable varieties may succumb to very wet conditions in autumn and winter. This is particularly true if you have very heavy soil.

Some growers may not supply your plants until summer; you should plant them on receipt, but do not expect a show of blooms until the following year. The advantage of summer planting is that the roots can get established in warm soil. Make sure you keep them well-watered, especially in hot, dry weather.

Plant delphiniums in groups of three or five, as odd numbers tend to look less regimented than even numbers.

The popular variety 'Butterball' (below right) has white flowers, cream eyes and an overall greenish-yellow tinge.

Belladonna varieties, such as 'Lamartine' (below) have more widely separated flowers.

For the best effect, plant groups of the same colour or variety together. Plant them at least 60cm/2ft apart.

Spoilt for choice

There are so many really gorgeous named varieties on offer from nurseries that it is impossible to suggest more than a tiny proportion of them here.

'Olive Poppleton' (1.8m/6ft tall) looks well at the back of borders and brings drama to a scheme. This variety has pure white petals and a honey brown 'bee' or eye in the centre of the flower.

To bring warmth to your garden choose one of the lovely dusky pink varieties. 'Royal Flush', also sold as 'Langdon's Royal Flush' (1.5m/5ft tall), is a deep, rich pink with a white, contrasting eye. Grey or silver foliage plants will complement this lovely variety.

A cream variety such as 'Butterball' (1.2m/4ft tall) is ideal for a classic colour scheme of pink, cream and fresh green foliage.

Nothing quite beats purple for bringing richness to your garden. Purple mixes well with other colours, particularly yellow or white. The grey-eyed six-footer, 'Gordon Forsyth', is a good choice.

Famous blues

Delphiniums are rightly famous for their blues, which range from very pale to very dark. A deep gentian blue can be had by planting 'Fenella' (1.8m/6ft) or 'Nicholas Woodfield'; both have black eyes.

For annual delphiniums (larkspur) choose 'Giant Imperial' or 'Hyacinth Flowered' mixtures. Larkspur is better for cutting and drying then perennial varieties and may be grown from seed in autumn or spring.

Perennial Belladonna varieties are single flowered and branching, which makes them good for cutting. Choose 'Lamartine' for a violet/blue. 'Piccolo' is a short-growing, free-flowering gentian blue and 'Moerheimii' is white.

Busy Lizzies

If you are looking for an easy, reliable annual to add colour to your garden throughout the summer, then the aptly-named busy Lizzie is the plant for you.

Everything about busy Lizzies suggests bright, cheerful bustle. This bushy, succulent-stemmed and almost perpetual-flowering plant was given its common name because of its fast growth and the persistence with which it flowers. Seedlings begin to produce blooms when they are only an inch or so tall, and carry on doing so all through the summer months.

Even its generic name, *Impatiens*, suggests swift movement, though in this case it is named not for its growth habits but rather for the speed with which it discharges its seeds when ripe.

Busy Lizzies are enormously versatile plants. Several different varieties planted together in a bed make a colourful ground cover (right), while a single variety will grace a tub or window-box (below). If they are left in their pots, other options arise. Wedging the pots in the gaps in a honeycomb wall, for example, enables the plants to make lovely vertical cover (opposite above).

A striking alternative to conventional busy Lizzies is provided by the new, larger-flowered New Guinea hybrids, some with variegated foliage (opposite below).

a pronounced spur at the back.

None of the new compact strains is likely to grow beyond a height of 30-40cm/12-15in, which makes them ideal candidates for hanging baskets, small tubs and window boxes, though they are equally good performers when planted out as summer bedding. They are extremely versatile and can safely be used in difficult, shady parts of the garden or in full sunshine: not many half-hardy annuals tolerate both conditions. There will, naturally, be more flowers if the plant is grown in full sun.

Among the many hybrid strains of *Impatiens* are plants with flowers of all shades of

The ancestral strains of *Impatiens* originated in the tropical and sub-tropical areas of Africa and the Far East.

From these tall, rangy ancestors have been developed a vast range of hybrids that have all of the good habits and none of the drawbacks of the parent plant. Most busy Lizzie hybrids are notable for their compact, low-growing habit and for their profuse blooming. The flowers are generally single, though there are some spectacular doubles, and have

PLANT PROFILE

Suitable site and soil Does well in full sun or partial shade. Will tolerate most soil conditions if kept moist, but not waterlogged.

Planting Plant out young specimens when all danger of frost has passed. Prepare the border by working in a little well-rotted garden compost and sprinkle in a handful of bone meal to enrich the area around the roots of each plant; they should be placed 15-23cm/6-9in apart. Water in.

Cultivation and care Require little attention apart from regular watering when the rain does not oblige.

Propagation If growing from seed, this should be sown indoors or under glass in spring. Use peat-based compost and cover the seeds lightly. Seedlings must be kept at a temperature of at least 18°C/65°.

When they are about 4cm/1½in high, transplant them into individual pots of loam-based compost. Alternatively, tip cuttings 5-8cm/2-3in long can be taken in summer or early autumn and rooted in water before being potted up.

Pests and diseases Slugs can be a problem to younger, weaker plants and aphids may occasionally take a fancy to the odd specimen.

Recommended varieties So many varieties have been developed that it is difficult to make a choice. Here are some to look out for.
- The fast-growing 'Imp' and 'Super Elfin' strains grown to around 23cm/9in high and produce large flowers in a full range of colours.
- 'Novette' mixture, with plants only 10cm/4in high, and 'Florette' (15cm/6in) are good for edging and for the front of mixed borders.
- 'Futura', which has a trailing habit, is ideal for window boxes and hanging baskets.
- 'Camellia flowered Mixed' (45cm/18in) and 'Tom Thumb Mixed' (20cm/10in) are best for the balsam-type double flowers; 'Confection Mixed' is the choice for conventional doubles.
- 'Zig-Zag', which has striped blooms, is extremely eye-catching, while 'Grand Prix' bears the largest flowers.

pink, red, orange, mauve and white. There are also bi-coloured varieties – for instance, red or pink striped with white.

The leaves may be elliptic or heart-shaped and can be coloured in almost every imaginable shade of green; some have a bronze or purple sheen and reddish or brown speckles on the undersides.

Named varieties

Although they are raised from named types, in garden centres you may be faced with rows of plants marked simply 'Impatiens F1 Hybrid', giving the colour and brief information on the height, spread and general care of the plant.

However, if you wish to look further into the various varieties, a specialist grower should be able to identify and supply a much wider range of named

Impatiens hybrids.

The best way to get a named variety, though, is to raise plants from seed. As a basic bedding plant for borders and large containers, it is difficult to beat the fast-growing 'Imp' and 'Super Elfin' varieties. Both grow to around 23cm/9in tall and produce large flowers in a full range of colours.

If you have smaller containers, try the dwarf 'Novette' mixture. This free-flowering variety grows to just 10cm/4in tall, making it a good choice for edging a border. The same is true of the slightly taller (15cm/6in) 'Florette' series.

The compact colour they provide make busy Lizzies a good choice for window boxes; the semi-pendulous habit of the 'Futura' variety makes it ideal for boxes and for hanging baskets, where it makes a good companion for trailing

Named varieties are not always available as bedding plants, but they can be raised from seed without much difficulty, and are well worth the effort. The striped blooms of 'Zig Zag' (left) make a striking display for a container or hanging basket, while the small blooms of the dwarf form, 'Novette Mixed' (below left) make excellent bedding plants for the front of a border. 'Super Elfin Mixed' (right) is a taller variety, with correspondingly larger flowers. Large flowers are also characteristic of the New Guinea hybrids; the pink and white blooms of 'Fanfare' (below right) are set off by handsomely variegated leaves. Impatiens F1 hybrids include several double-flowered varieties. Although some are named, others are simply sold as 'Double Mixed' (below). Sometimes the double flowers resemble roses; others are more open.

pelargoniums, fuchsias, petunias and lobelia.

Complex double varieties, no less free-flowering, are available for those who want to put on a little more show in their borders.

The camellia-flowered busy Lizzies (which are usually called balsam, the name under which you will find them in some catalogues) are varieties of *I. balsamina*, and come in shades of rose, blush pink, scarlet and white. 'Camellia Flowered Mixed', one of the largest busy Lizzie varieties, grows to 45cm/18in. The same type of showy flower can be had in smaller plants; try 'Tom Thumb Mixed' (25cm/10in).

There are double-flowered forms of the more conventional busy Lizzie, too, such as 'Confection Mixed' (20-30cm/8-12in tall, with fine, double and semi-double flowers).

Growing busy Lizzies

Strictly speaking, *Impatiens* is a perennial. Growers of houseplants will be well aware of the busy Lizzie's sterling service indoors – a well cared for specimen can be kept at peak performance for years.

However, when grown as a garden plant in temperate conditions it must be regarded as a tender half-hardy annual. Most modern *Impatiens* hybrids are started off in spring under glass and discarded in the autumn before the first frosts puts paid to them. Young plants can be purchased through mail-order catalogues and begin to appear in garden centres in late spring.

They may, of course, be propagated from seed at home, though this will have to be done indoors, as seedlings must be kept at a minimum temperature of 18°C/65°F.

Seed should be sown on a growing medium based on peat or a peat substitute in spring and lightly covered. When the seedlings are large enough to handle (about 4cm/1½in tall), transplant them into individual pots of loam-based compost. Pinch out the growing tips of young plants regularly to ensure bushiness.

Alternatively, you can take tip cuttings 5-8cm/2-3in long from existing plants in the summer and root them in water. Transfer them to a soil-based compost when roots 1½cm/½in long have formed, and over-winter them indoors.

Whole plants can also be lifted from the garden and

NEW BLOOMS

Striking new hybrids with larger flowers have recently been developed as a result of a plant-gathering expedition to New Guinea. Some strains reputedly produce flowers over 8cm/3in across. Many of the most colourful have strongly variegated foliage.

These New Guinea hybrids are now becoming available through garden centres and mail-order catalogues.

The camellia flowered busy Lizzies (above) are varieties of I. balsamina and are often sold as balsam. Unlike other Impatiens hybrids, they are true annuals. Most varieties have an upright growth habit, and do not branch. While the species has small, single flowers, hybrids are fully double; the flower stems are very short and the blooms appear to burst out from between the lance-shaped leaves.

INDOOR PESTS

When you are raising plants indoors, they can be susceptible to pests which also enjoy the warm conditions. This is especially true if you have a large collection of houseplants.

Red spider mite can be a real menace if conditions become very dry, causing mottling and bronzing of leaves, which may begin to drop.

Whitefly is another nuisance. It disfigures and weakens the plants. In each case, treat with a suitable systemic insecticide such as dimethoate.

then over-wintered indoors. Usually, though, they have become so leggy by the end of the summer that they are not worth hanging on to.

Planting out

Whichever method of propagation you choose, or whether you simply decide to start again with new plantlets each year, do take care not to plant them out too early. Always harden them off gradually, accustoming them to lower temperatures and more airy conditions for a week or two before planting them out in their final positions.

Once the danger of their main enemy, frost, is past, busy Lizzies could not be ea-

sier to grow. There are, however, always the usual garden pests around, ready to prey on vulnerable individuals.

Slugs and snails may attack seedlings and young plants, especially in periods of wet weather. A sprinkling of slug pellets from time to time should keep them at bay.

Also, keep an eye out for infestations of aphids on leaves or stems, which will weaken the plants, make them sticky and encourage mould.

Once summer is under way, all you really need to do is keep your plants well-watered, and they will reward you with a heartening display of colour throughout the season and well into the autumn.

Daisy, Daisy

The golden composite flower heads and rayed petals of Michaelmas daisies bring a welcome late flush of colour to the garden.

As the summer winds down into autumn, most flowering plants in the garden are past their best. The Michaelmas daisy, though, is just coming into its own, bringing a mass of colour to the border. Most varieties are free-flowering, and produce heads of golden-hearted, daisy-like flowers with petals in vibrant shades of pink, white, red, blue and violet.

The flowering season lasts a couple of months, from late summer until well into the autumn. This late flush of colourful blooms proves a boon not only to the gardener, but also to garden wildlife; bees and butterflies about to go into hibernation find the plants an invaluable source of nectar to fortify them through their long winter sleep.

Composite flowers

Michaelmas daisies are asters, a large genus of late-flowering herbaceous perennials. Like

All asters have colourful, daisy-like flowers, but some are more colourful and prolific than others. The compact, bushy Aster amellus 'King George' (above) grows to a height and spread of 50cm/20in and is smothered in blooms throughout the autumn.

63

other 'daisy-flowered' plants, asters are members of a large botanical family which includes plants as different as the meadow daisy (*Bellis perennis*) and the sunflower.

All these plants have composite flower heads made up of many tiny individual florets surrounded, in their single forms, by a ring of petals. In the semi-double forms, the array of petals becomes much thicker, swelling to a mop of colour which all but hides the composite centre in the fully double varieties.

Strictly speaking, the name 'Michaelmas daisy' applies only to hybrids developed from a single species, *Aster novi-belgii*. Several varieties, such as 'Fellowship', with large, pink, double flowers, the pale blue 'Climax' and 'Royal Velvet', whose blooms are a rich, sumptuous violet, grow to around 1.2m/4ft tall or more. These tall varieties may require staking and are primarily decorative plants for the back of a border.

More often grown today are the many dwarf hybrids, between 30cm/1ft and 90cm/3ft tall, which can be used in the middle or front of a border. These include fairly substantial plants, such as 'Carnival', which carries its rich pinkish-red blooms 60-75cm/2-2½ft high, and true dwarfs such as the white 'Snowsprite', just 30cm/1ft tall. In between are

The New England aster, A. novae-angliae *'Harrington's Pink' (top) has clear, rose-pink, many-petalled blooms that stand out dazzlingly against the rather dull green of its foliage. By contrast, another* A. novae-angliae *variety, 'September Ruby' (above), despite the richer petal colour and the bright, golden centres of its blooms, has much brighter leaves, giving a softer overall effect.*

garden favourites such as 'Little Pink Beauty' and the pale blue 'Audrey'.

New England asters

Almost indistinguishable from *Aster novi-belgii* is another American species, *A. novae-angliae*, known in the USA, and occasionally elsewhere, as New England asters. They grow very tall, regularly reaching 1.5m/5ft, and sometimes topping 1.8m/6ft, making them perfect subjects for the back of the border. Their

good, late-flowering perennials. *A. thomsonii* (also spelled *thompsonii*) comes from the Himalayas. It produces a profusion of lavender-blue flowers and is best-known in the dwarf variety 'Nanus', growing to 45cm/18in.

Species asters

Aster × frikartii is a cross between *A. amellus* and *A. thomsonii*. Its attractive flowers are a cool lavender blue, with needle thin petals. It has a particularly long flowering season and is tolerant of poor conditions, though like all asters it prefers a well-drained, yet water-retentive soil. It thrives on chalk.

Not often seen, but worth looking out for, is *Aster lateriflorus* 'Horizontalis', which forms a compact, twiggy bush,

RECOMMENDED VARIETIES

Specialist nurseries often stock literally hundreds of aster varieties, most of them specific to a single grower. Many garden centres also carry a confusingly wide range. Ultimately, it is a question of colour and individual preference, though there are some varieties which have remained popular over the course of time.
A. novi-belgii Dwarf varieties; 'Little Pink Beauty' (pink), 'Audrey' (semi-double pale blue), 'Snowsprite' (white semi-double), 'Lady in Blue' (rich blue semi-double). Tall varieties; 'Fellowship' (large, pink double flowers), 'Royal Velvet' (violet), 'Royal Ruby' (deep red), 'Climax' (pale blue). Medium height; 'Winston S. Churchill' (ruby-red double), 'Carnival' (rich pinkish-red semi-double).
A. novae-angliae; 'Harrington's Pink' (pink), 'September Ruby' (rich red).
A. amellus: 'King George' (violet), 'Sonia' (pink), 'Mauve Beauty' (mauve).
A. thomsonii 'Nanus' (pale lavender-blue).
A. × frikartii 'Mönch' (bright blue with striking orange-yellow centre).

colour range includes various shades of pink, crimson, mauve and blue.

'September Ruby' is an excellent, free-flowering variety with rich red petals and a golden centre. 'Harrington's Pink' is equally prolific, but with rosy-coloured blooms.

An Italian species, *Aster amellus*, is less well known than *A. novi-belgii*, but deserves greater prominence. It shares many of the attractions of *A. novi-belgii* hybrids but usually lives longer and is not

Hybrids of the **Erigeron** *genus produce flowers with a striking similarity to asters, but they appear in spring and summer rather than autumn. 'Felicity' (top) produces a splendid bush of pink daisy-like flowers.*

The double flowers of **A. novi-belgii** *'Winston S Churchill' (above) combine petals of a rich ruby red with a markedly golden centre in a truly vibrant colour scheme.*

as susceptible to disease.

Varieties of *A. amellus* tend to have single flowers, larger than most Michaelmas daisies, in shades of pink, mauve and violet. They make compact plants, rarely exceeding a height and spread of 60cm/2ft.

The very free-flowering 'King George', which has violet blooms, is the best-known variety; the pink 'Sonia' also finds a home in many gardens, while 'Mauve Beauty' lives up to its name.

Several other asters make

ANNUAL ASTERS

True asters are often confused with China asters, half-hardy annuals that are hybrids of *Callistephus chinensis.* Smaller than Michaelmas daisies – most varieties grow to 25-50cm/ 10-20in – they are in bloom at the same time and produce similar daisy-like composite flowers in a range of colours from white, through yellow, pinks and reds to blue and purple.

Many of them are chrysanthemum-flowered; double, single and pompon varieties are also available, some of them bi-coloured. Better varieties include the disease-resistant double 'Bouquet Powder Puffs', and the chrysanthemum-flowered 'Ostrich Plume' or 'Duchess Mixed'. 'Lilliput Mixed' is a good dwarf variety.

60cm/2ft high and 45cm/1½ft in diameter, smothered in the autumn with tiny flowers, mostly white, though some shading to pink, all with rich pink centres. As an added bonus, the leaves turn in the autumn, taking on a bronze hue with a hint of purple.

Alpine asters

There is an Alpine species, *A. alpinus*, which comes in shades of blue and mauve; it is smaller – just 15cm/6in tall – and much less free-flowering than other asters, carrying each delicate bloom on a single stem, and is really suitable only for rockery cultivation. *A. alpinus* is summer-flowering,

FEEDING

Generally speaking, Michaelmas daisies do not need a great deal of special attention. They do appreciate a feed in late winter; spread garden compost or another organic mulch around the plants and hoe it in. If the plants seem to run out of strength in mid-summer, repeat the dose.

GO ORGANIC!

as are one or two worthwhile lesser-known species, such as *A. yunnanensis*.

Those who want a summer-flowering 'Michaelmas daisy', however, would do better to try one of the various hybrids in the related *Erigeron* genus. These perennials have delightful daisy-like flowers in shades of pink, lilac, violet and mauve, and make compact plants, 45-60cm/1½-2ft high, that flower through the summer months. 'Felicity' is a delightful soft pink, while 'Darkest of All', as its name suggests, is a deep violet.

Growth and care

Michaelmas daisies and the other widely-grown asters are relatively easy plants to grow. Once established, they need little care beyond a regular watering and an annual feed.

They are difficult to raise from seed – though paradoxically often self-seed – and are best propagated by division in spring or autumn or by taking

soft cuttings in spring. These should be rooted in pots and planted out in autumn. Plants purchased from garden centres can be planted out when they are bought.

The plants look best planted in small groups; three is an ideal number. Taller varieties should be staked.

Michaelmas daisies can cope with any soil but prefer fertile, water-retentive ground, even heavy clays. They happily tolerate damp positions on the banks of rivers and ponds as well as thriving in borders. In fact, the only condition with which they cannot cope is drought in the growing season. They must be watered regularly in dry weather.

Michaelmas daisies, in fact all asters, make excellent cut flowers. If you do not harvest the blooms regularly, be sure to dead-head the plant to ensure repeat flowering. Once they have stopped flowering, cut the plants back close to the ground to help new growth.

Varieties of **Callistephus chinensis** *are sold as annual asters. 'Ostrich Plume Mixed' (left, above) is typical of the colour range.*

A. thomsonii 'Nana' (left, below) is among the best dwarf asters. The tiny blooms of A. lateriflorus *'Horizontalis' (below) are borne aloft on woody branches.*

GROWING TIPS

PINCHING OUT

Left to themselves, Michaelmas daisies will make a tall, straggly clump, with each stem carrying heads of flowers. You can make them more compact and encourage the production of flowering stems by pinching out the growing tips in early summer.

SEASONAL PLANTING

Ideally, cuttings should be planted out in the autumn. In practice, however, they can be put into their flowering positions as soon as they have developed a reasonable root system. Plants bought from garden centres, for instance, are usually raised from cuttings, and they should go in the ground as soon as possible after purchase.

Certainly, if you are going on holiday in the summer, your aster cuttings stand a better chance of fending for themselves if they are established in the border before you leave. Cuttings in pots will dry out much more quickly than those in the ground.

DON'T FORGET!

PERFECT PARTNERS

Michaelmas daisies prolong the interest in a mixed bed into the autumn. Here, a pink and a red variety are coming into full flower as the lavatera and fuschia begin to fade. A late-flowering tobacco plant, Nicotiana alata 'Lime Green', keeps them company.

Miniature Roses

Gardeners find roses irresistible for their beauty and long flowering season. Miniatures have the same charms, plus the appeal of all things tiny.

The small size of many new gardens, and the increasing trend towards container planting, have led to a considerable increase in the popularity of miniature roses. Their tiny, dainty flowers have an appeal all of their own, and the small-sized plants – sometimes no more than 20cm/8in high – enable rose lovers to plant a pleasing selection where there is no room for ordinary full-size rose bushes.

Miniatures offer everything desirable in a rose – they are all repeat flowering, with a long season of bloom, and many are fragrant. The varieties available offer all the range of beautiful colours found in their larger cousins; reds, oranges, pinks, whites, yellows, lilac, bi-colours and even a near-green. The flowers are almost always double, and the plants themselves, despite their delicate appearance, are perfectly hardy.

The term miniature rose encompasses two distinct types: true miniatures and slightly larger plants that are sometimes catalogued as patio roses. There are also a few climbing miniature roses, and some varieties are also available as standards, growing a single straight stem about 30cm/1ft high.

Potted history

The miniature rose is not a new introduction – they were very popular in Victorian days, but gradually fell out of fashion and had all but disappeared by 1900.

Then, in 1918, a Major Roulet happened on a tiny pot-grown rose in Switzerland, which became known as *Rosa rouletii*. From this small beginning came the legions of present-day miniature roses.

Miniature roses are extremely popular in the United States, where they are used as house plants. In Britain, they do not succeed very well indoors, and many people became disillusioned with them.

Many miniature roses are versions of well-known varieties: the colouring of 'Baby Masquerade' (above) mimics that of its grown-up sister.

The glossy foliage of 'Snow Carpet', also known as 'Maccarpe' (right) makes dense ground cover, and it flowers into the autumn.

The delightful double pink flowers of 'Pompon de Paris' (far right) were favourites of the Victorians.

The razmataz of the semi-double blooms of 'Stars 'n' Stripes' (right) would probably be overwhelming in a full-size rose, but makes for an appealingly colourful, candy-striped focus in a miniature form.

PLANT PROFILE

Suitable site and soil
Well-prepared fertile soil in full sun.

Planting Buy container-grown roses for planting in spring or early summer, or bare root stock for planting from the beginning of autumn to late winter. Place the plants 20cm/8in to 40cm/15in apart, depending on the effect required.

Cultivation and care Treat as ordinary roses, but don't forget to water well in dry weather as they have much smaller root systems and so dry out faster. Plants grown in pots and tubs may need watering twice a day in warm weather. Feed frequently with liquid fertilizer. Snip off dead blooms to encourage further flowering. Prune lightly at the beginning of spring – just

remove any dead wood and trim plant to desired shape. Plants can be brought indoors temporarily when in flower if desired, but should be promptly returned to the garden after they have finished flowering.

Propagation Take 7.5cm/3in cuttings from new growth in early autumn. Put several in a pot and keep out of direct sunlight. When new growth appears, pot up separately in 7.5cm/3in pots. Keep indoors until spring, then plant out or keep in pots – cuttings make good house plants.

Pests and diseases Watch for aphids and spray as soon as any appear. Like other roses, miniatures may also suffer from mildew and black spot. Spray at the first signs of disease – remove and burn all black-spotted leaves.

The reason is that the plants are raised differently. In the USA they are grown from cuttings, which makes them slow-growing and not very hardy, but guarantees they will remain small. In Britain the plants are generally grafted on to rootstocks of larger roses. This makes them hardier, faster-growing, and suited to life outdoors – but also means they can eventually grow undesirably large.

Ancient and modern

As with full-size roses, some miniature varieties have been in cultivation for a very long time. The bright pink 'Pompon de Paris', for example, was very popular in Victorian times. Others date back to the 1940s, but most of the big sellers are modern roses, produced by hybridists in the 1970s and 1980s. They are very fond of naming their babies after British TV personalities – if you wish you can buy 'Anna Ford', 'Angela Rippon' and 'Penelope Keith'.

One of the very latest patio roses is 'Queen Mother', launched in 1990 to celebrate Her Majesty's 90th birthday. This has semi-double flowers

across, but can sometimes be as big as 5cm/2in, and are almost always double.

Like their big sisters, miniatures produce flowers of varying shape and habit of growth. Depending on their parentage they may resemble miniature floribundas, growing in clusters, or tiny hybrid teas with high-centred blooms: many have rosette or pompon-type flowers. Some are mildly fragrant, but many of the new ones have no scent. The leaves are similar to those of big roses, but in proportion to the size of the plant, and the stems are usually prickly.

There are also patio roses, larger and somewhere between a miniature and a floribunda rose in character. Their average height is around 45cm/18in, and they have a neat, bushy habit of growth. Some nurseries do not list patio roses separately from miniatures, so check heights carefully when buying or you may end up with something which is three times larger than you had envisaged.

Buying miniatures

As they become popular, more garden centres are stocking a selection of miniature and patio roses. But for a really good choice you need to go to a specialist rose nursery, or send away for a catalogue so you can buy by mail order.

If possible see plants in bloom before buying, or at least in a colour photograph – they vary a lot in character, and what appeals to one person may not please another. For example, a popular patio rose, 'Chelsea Pensioner', is described as deep scarlet with gold shading at the base of the petals. In real life what you see is a startling mixture of scarlet and pink, because the flowers fade as they age.

Using miniatures

Miniature roses have a long flowering season, coming into bloom in midsummer and car-

in a delightful soft pink shade, and a very dainty, delicate appearance. If you are looking for something really unusual, there's even a pale, creamy green-flowered miniature – it's called 'Green Diamond'.

Little and large

A truly miniature rose grows no more than 20-30cm/8-12in tall – a few are listed as reaching only 15cm/6in. The flowers are usually about 2.5cm/1in

The distinction between miniature varieties and patio roses is not clear-cut; 'Dresden Doll' (above) is listed as a miniature in most catalogues, but a patio rose in others.

Miniature roses are versatile performers. Patio roses in containers make excellent specimen plants for a patio (above left), while several genuine miniature varieties make a vigorous show in a raised bed (below left).

'Yellow Doll' (below) is a genuine miniature, but there is nothing small or self-effacing about its magnificent double yellow blooms.

CAREFUL PLANTING

Plant your miniature roses with great care, otherwise they will never flourish.

Container grown Dig a hole in moist soil large enough for the container plus a 7.5cm/3in layer of proprietary planting mixture or moist peat all round and underneath. Do not use garden soil as roots raised in peat-based compost in the container may not move out into it. The top of the container should be at ground level. Gently slit and remove the container; do not break up compost around the roots. Set on the planting mixture and fill the space all round. Firm down well and water in.

Bare root Make a hole broad enough to give the roots plenty of room and deep enough to allow the bump where the grafted plants joins the rootstock to be 2.5cm/1in below ground. Fill with proprietary planting mixture and tread firmly. Keep moist until established.

DON'T FORGET!

rying on right until the first frosts strike. They are also extremely versatile.

Use them to create a small-scale rose garden, ideally in a raised bed so that they are closer to the eye. A mixture of true miniatures with the larger patio roses at the back or in the centre will give you the height gradation that makes a bed look as though it is professionally laid out.

Rockery roses

Alternatively, you can put some miniatures in a rockery to give interest in summer when many of the alpine flowers are long gone.

True miniatures, closely planted, make excellent edgings for conventional borders, while the slightly larger patio roses are recommended for container planting. However, once again it is a matter of scale, and a lot depends on the size of the container. Both sizes are ideal for beds and containers around a patio, where they can be seen at close quarters and really appreciated.

The one thing **not** to do with miniatures is mix them up with larger plants, especially full-size roses, or their small-scale charms will be much overshadowed and lost.

Lilies

Despite their exotic appearance, many lilies are perfectly hardy plants that will reward a little care with a long-lasting, spectacular display of flowers.

Lilies are among the most aristocratic of all garden plants, bearing their large, strikingly shaped flowers aloft on a single tall and stately stem. The flowers are often graced with exotic spots and stripes, and there are varieties in every colour bar blue.

Because lilies are so remarkably beautiful, they are considered difficult to grow, and they do generally need a little more care than more commonplace plants. But the lily family is a vast one, and far from all of its members are overly demanding. Over the last 50 years lily breeders have produced many new hybrids which are hardier and more disease-resistant than the parents, and possessed of even more magnificent flowers.

Magnificent obsession

Growing lilies is so fascinating that many gardeners become addicted, studying catalogues avidly each spring and autumn and gradually amassing large collections, featuring every lily that will flourish in their particular garden.

Although some lilies can grow very tall – the leopard lily (*Lilium pardalinum*) can exceed 2.4m/8ft – the single erect stems do not take up a lot of elbow room, so they are well suited to small gardens where they can be studied at close quarters in all their splendour. Many varieties also look well in a patio tub.

Many people are put off buying lilies because the bulbs are relatively expensive – several pounds for a single bulb in some cases. But for a small

PLANT PROFILE

Suitable site and soil
Sheltered but well-ventilated spot, usually sunny, though some prefer shade. Roots must always be in shade. Rich well-drained soil – most lilies prefer acid or neutral soil, but a few tolerate or even prefer lime.

Planting Plant in spring or autumn, as soon as possible after purchase to reduce risk of drying out. If bulbs look shrivelled, keep in moist peat for 10 days first. Work coarse grit or sand into the soil to improve drainage, if necessary. Set bulb so that tip is 2½ times its height below soil level – about 7.5cm/3in for small bulbs, 10-20cm/4-8in for larger ones. Set stem-rooting lilies more deeply, and *L. candidum* and *L. × testacum*

with the tips almost showing. Plant about 23cm/9in apart, depending on ultimate height. Mark planting spot with a stick.

Cultivation and care Mulch after planting and replace regularly. Protect newly planted lilies from frost with a covering of peat. Water in dry weather, avoiding leaves. Tall plants may need staking. Cut off the flower spike when the blooms have withered.

Propagation Divide mature plants in autumn every 3-4 years, or plant bulblets or bulbils if produced.

Pests and diseases Prone to attack by a large number of pests, fungi and viruses, but spraying at the first sign of trouble will control most of them. Use wildlife-safe pellets to deter slugs.

There is plenty of choice in lily species. L. hansonii (left) has pendent orange blooms. The white petals of L. auratum (above) are up to 18cm/7in long, while the turk's caps of L. martagon (below) are smaller. The white Madonna lily (L. candidum), yellow L. 'Citronella' and orange lily make a vibrant group (right).

garden, where quality should take precedence over quantity, the expense is more than justified by the results. Besides, once they are established, most lilies will spread, and after a few years they can very easily be divided up to produce several new plants.

A historic plant

Lilies have been cultivated for literally thousands of years. One of the best known, the pure white Madonna lily (*Lilium candidum*), was almost certainly brought to Britain by the Romans, and by medieval times had become a symbol of Christianity and the special flower of the Virgin Mary. Even today it is widely used to decorate churches.

In more recent times, the lily-lover's focus has switched from Europe to Asia, and particularly to China. The famous plant hunter, Ernest Henry Wilson, found *Lilium regale* growing in an inaccessible val-

L. hansonii (orange-yellow turk's cap)
L. henryi (yellow turk's cap)
L. martagon (rose-purple, spotted turk's cap)
L. pyrenaicum (greenish-yellow turk's cap)
L. regale (white funnels flushed pink)
L. tigrinum also known as *L. lancifolium*
(orange-red turk's cap)
'Black Dragon' (trumpets, white inside, dark red outside)
'Bright Star' (white cups with orange stripe)
'Casablanca' (large white cups)
'Citronella' (lemon to golden yellow)
'Connecticut King' (bright yellow cups)
'Enchantment' (orange-red cups with black spots)
'Green Dragon' (white cups streaked brown and green outside)
'Harlequin' strain (all colours)
'Pink Perfection' (pink trumpets)
'Star Gazer' (crimson-red with white border)

ley in tens of thousands – its heady fragrance must have been overpowering.

Fascinating flowers

There is a tremendous variation in lily flowers. Although always recognizable as lilies, they appear in no less than six different shapes.

Those that have bell-shaped flowers, such as *L. nanum*, have petals that are either straight or curve inwards towards the tips. In bowl-shaped flowers (*L. auratum*, for exam-

The nodding, scarlet turk's cap blooms of L. pumilum, *also known as* L. tenuifolium *(right) are among the smallest of all true lily flowers.*

After a few years, if all goes well, your lilies should have spread into a large clump. To increase your stock, dig the clump up in autumn, and break it apart into groups of bulbs. Replant immediately, so that the bulbs will have time to grow new roots before winter comes.

If your lily produces bulbils in the leaf axils, or bulblets on the underground stem, detach these in autumn and replant immediately in a nursery bed. Keep them there for two years before moving to permanent quarters.

GROWING TIPS

ple), the petals are more widely spaced and slightly recurved or reflexed (that is, rolled back) at the tips.

Cup- or star-shaped flowers, as in the hybrid 'Bright Star', are similar but more compact, and may or may not roll back at the tips. *L. regale* has funnel-shaped flowers. These are more tubular, flaring out towards the mouth. Trumpet-shaped flowers, like those of the popular Easter lily (*L. longiflorum*) are the same but longer and narrower.

Perhaps the best-known flower form is the turk's cap or martagon type, with strongly recurved petals – sometimes so much so that the flower becomes actually ball shaped and the long, graceful stamens are fully exposed.

This is not the end of the lily flowers' variety. While some are pendent, nodding their heads to the ground, others point outwards, or upwards to face the sun.

Many lilies add to their attractiveness with a rich fragrance, although some, such as *L. pyrenaicum*, actually smell rather unpleasant.

Most lilies flower in midsummer, but some flower earlier or later, so it is perfectly possible to have a succession of lilies blooming in your garden for almost half the year.

The flowers are produced at the top of a single upright stem, grouped in pairs or bunches. The number of flowers can be up to 50 or more, and they appear over a period of several weeks. They vary in size from the modest 2.5cm/1in blooms of *L. pumilum* to those produced by the golden-rayed lily (*L. auratum*), which can reach 30cm/12in across. Lily leaves are stalkless and relatively insignificant, growing in whorls or scattered evenly up the stem.

True and false lilies

All true lilies – members of the genus *Lilium* – grow from bulbs. This distinguishes them

Many years of work by dedicated lily lovers have produced some truly spectacular varieties and hybrids. The tiger lily (L. lancifolium syn. L. tigrinum), with its large, spotted turk's cap flowers, has long been a favourite; the variety L. l. splendens (above) has even bigger flowers in a brighter shade of orange.

PERFECT PARTNERS

The pale, shapely blooms of the Madonna lily are an excellent foil for colourful border plants. Here they set off the pale pinks and yellows of *Alstroemeria* 'Ligtu'.

The golden yellow cups of the hybrid 'Connecticut King' (left) are held aloft on stems some 1m/3ft high with their faces to the sun.

LILIES IN CONTAINERS

Growing lilies in containers means that you can put them somewhere inconspicuous while they are developing, and move them into the limelight when in flower. Do not forget, though, that very large containers become too heavy to move once filled with compost.

Container growing also means that you have full control over the type of soil, and the position, to suit the lily's needs.

Add interest by planting a small companion plant around the lily – this will help keep the bulbs cool by shading the soil. Choose small annuals in a colour that complements the lily. Use white flowers, or grey-leaved plants such as senecio, to cool down a very brightly coloured lily.

from plants like arum lily (*Zantedeschia*) and day lily (*Hemerocallis*). The bulbs are different from ordinary ones like those of the daffodil, having no papery covering, and consisting of a large number of fleshy scales.

Like the flowers, the bulb shapes vary – some are round and some shaped like the rhizome of an iris, while others produce chains of round bulbs linked by stolons.

Many lilies produce bulblets on the underground part of the stem, just above the bulb. A few produce bulbils where the leaves join the stem. Both can be used for propagation.

Where to plant

Lilies can be grown in many parts of the garden. Those that like full sun thrive in herbaceous or mixed borders, or in tubs. Those that prefer dappled shade are excellent for planting under trees, or can be used among shrubs to provide

The funnel-shaped flowers of L. regale *are pink in bud, but open to a dazzling white (far left).*

'Enchantment' (left) *has become a popular cut flower in recent years. Very like the tiger lily in colour, it is distinguished by its upturned, cup-shaped flower form.*

The flowers of L. pyrenaicum *are lovely to look at (below left), but many find their scent unpleasant.*

Cardiocrinum giganteum (below), *sold as a giant lily, produces a tall, flamboyant flower spike, then the bulb dies, producing offsets that will flower again in five years.*

LILY CLASSIFICATIONS

Botanists divide the vast family of lilies into nine groups. The largest contains all the original species lilies found growing wild in different parts of the world, many of which are hardy and easily grown. The other eight contain the huge number (over 3,500 registered!) of hybrids – some hardy, some tender – which have developed by crossing and recrossing the species plants. The six main groups readily available to gardeners are listed below.
● **Asiatic hybrids** are generally compact, no more than 1.2m/4ft high. Many are unfussy as to soil and aspect. The Mid-century hybrids contained within this group are especially easy.
● **Martagon and *L. hansonii* hybrids** all have small, pendent, turk's cap flowers and do best in partial shade.
● **Candidum and *L. chalcedonicum* hybrids** have long, pendent, trumpet-shaped flowers.
● **Bellingham hybrids** do best on acid soil in semi-shade.
● **Trumpet and Aurelian hybrids** mostly have large, trumpet-shaped flowers. They prefer rich, lime-free soil and semi-shade.
● **Oriental hybrids** have striking white, crimson or pink flowers, but may not be quite so hardy as others; they are good subjects for tubs in the sun.

colour when these have finished flowering.

Plant lilies singly or in groups of three, in a spot where they can be admired at close quarters – though of course the really tall ones will need to go in the back of a border. If you grow several varieties, for the best effect keep them apart from one another.

Secrets of success

It is best to buy lily bulbs from specialist nurseries by mail order. They are normally despatched between autumn and spring – if the ground is frozen, plunge the bulbs into moist peat and wait. It is best not to choose a lily just for its looks – you **must** be able to give it the right conditions.

Most lilies offered by nurseries thrive in free-draining but not dry soil – work coarse sand or grit into heavier soils before planting lilies – and in sun or partial shade. Make sure that those preferring alkaline or acid soils get what they want – plant them in tubs if necessary. Good air circulation is needed, to avoid fungal infection – but strong winds can badly damage the plants.

Observe the recommended planting depth exactly, and mark the spot with a stick so that you remember where they are. (Also do this when the stems die down in autumn, so there is no risk of digging up or damaging the precious bulbs while they are dormant.)

In winter, avoid frost damage to lilies in borders by mulching thickly with peat; bring containers into a frost-free shed. Protect bulbs from snails and slugs, and keep watch for aphids, which can spread virus diseases.

SUPERLILY

GARDEN NOTES

Some lily nurseries also offer *Cardiocrinum giganteum*, a species of giant lily. The bulbs are among the most expensive, but a giant lily in full flower is a real talking point. The stem grows to 2.4m/8ft high or more, and each one can carry 25 flowers. These are 15-20cm/6-8in long, pure white trumpets, striped reddish purple inside, and give way to decorative seed heads.

Anemones

The charming anemones bought from florists enjoy an enduring popularity, but they are just one member of a large, easy-going family of attractive garden flowers.

When people think of anemones, they usually picture the cheerful and colourful blooms bought by the bunch at florists. These delightful plants have long been favourites because of their simple, cup-shaped flowers and the vibrant richness of their colours. However, there are many other types of anemone that are less well-known but just as stunning in their own way.

Hardy and versatile

All anemones are perennial; some grow from tubers or corms, others grow from creeping rhizomes. Some are frost hardy, which means that they will tolerate winter temperatures of −5°C/23°F, and some are fully hardy, which means that they can withstand temperatures as low as −15°C/5°F. Their perennial nature and general toughness make them an excellent choice for any garden.

Anemones are a versatile family. It is possible to have anemones of one sort or another blooming in your garden from early spring until well into autumn. There are even ones that will fill those awkward semi-shaded spots near hedges and walls. They can find homes in herbaceous borders, rock gardens, woodland areas or even on windowsills in or outside the house.

Colourful charmers

The most widely known anemones are varieties of the species *Anemone coronaria*. Their gorgeous colours make them instantly recognizable. These lovely plants come in two main

types, the De Caen series and the St. Brigid series.

Both produce cup-shaped flowers. If you cut dead flowers back to soil level you may be rewarded with a succession of up to 20 flowers per plant, provided conditions are right. Just dig in plenty of well-rotted humus and follow the

planting instructions carefully and you could get lots of flowers for your money.

Most garden centres sell the corms of De Caen and St. Brigid in packets of mixed colours. These include reds, deep blues or purples, various pinks and plain white. It is possible to buy named varieties in

The anemones commonly sold as cut flowers are the 'De Caen' series of Anemone coronaria (above). These vibrantly-coloured, single, spring blooms are available in named varieties, but are more commonly sold in packets of mixed colours.

single colours. You may have to search around a bit to do this, but it will be worth it if you have a specific colour scheme in mind.

The main difference between De Caen and St. Brigid is size of flower. De Caen flowers are single, with between 5 and 8 large petals while those of the St. Brigid series are larger and variously described as double or semi-double, depending on whose catalogue you read; strictly, they are semi-double.

Varieties of *A. coronaria* are frost hardy and enjoy open, sunny sites and good drainage. Plant tubers in bold groups for the best effect. Height can be anything from 5-25cm/2-10in, depending on the variety. You will probably have to replace them in a few years as plants tend to get weak after a while.

Eastern promise

The Japanese anemone (variously known as *A.* × *hybrida* or *A. japonica*) is considered by many to be one of the most beautiful of garden plants.

Vigorous, fully hardy and with a branching habit, it blooms from late summer to early autumn, bridging that awkward gap between early and late bloomers. Flowers may be single, semi-double or double. 'Honorine Jobert' has lovely, pure white flowers while others are various shades of pink. 'Max Vogel' tends towards mauve in colour and 'Prince Henry' is a deep, intensely rich pink.

Some varieties can grow to a height of 1.5m/5ft in favourable conditions and make good subjects for sites towards the back of the border. Others are shorter and can be placed to advantage in the centre or even at the front of a bed.

Japanese anemones look well backed by shrubs or planted with ornamental grasses, where their delicate flowers are shown off perfectly.

Sometimes described as doubles, the flowers of the 'St Brigid' series of A. coronaria *(top) are accurately called semi-double, despite their abundant petals, as their centres are open.*

PERFECT PARTNERS

Anemones' free-flowering nature is useful in schemes employing blocks of colour. Here, A. blanda *'White Splendour' combines dramatically with red tulips.*

Easily propagated in late autumn from root cuttings, they do well in partial shade and are good subjects for chalky or limy soils. Choose your site carefully; they tend to spread rather freely.

Small treasures

Varieties of *A. blanda* are small (height 5-10cm/4-6in) and fully hardy. They grow from knobbly tubers and produce star-shaped flowers with narrow petals in early spring. 'White Splendour' enjoys full sun, good drainage and humus-rich soil. 'Radar' has deep carmine flowers and will tolerate partial shade. 'Atrocaerulea' has deep blue flowers and likes good drainage and partial shade.

Anemone blanda varieties are easily propagated by dividing tubers when the leaves

have died back in early winter. They also seed themselves freely. All varieties look good planted at the edge of mixed or herbaceous borders.

Shady characters

There are several species of anemone that will take to life in shaded and moist areas. *A. nemorosa* varieties are commonly known as wood anemones because they thrive in woodland conditions. This means partial or dappled shade and rich, well-rotted leaf mould at the roots. Such conditions also tend to be on the damp side.

There are several varieties to choose from, the most popular being the simple, star-

RECOMMENDED VARIETIES

- *A. coronaria.* De Caen Series bear single flowers and St. Brigid Series larger ones. Both come in bright colours including white, cerise, blue/purple and red. Good named varieties include 'Mr Fokker' (deep bluish purple) and 'Hollandia' (fiery red).
- *A. blanda.* Varieties include 'Atrocaerulea' (dark blue), 'Pink Star' and 'Charmer' (pink) and 'Radar' (magenta). For a clear white with a pale yellow centre, choose 'White Splendour'.
- *A. × hybrida* or *A. japonica.* 'Bressingham Glow' (semi-double rosy-red). 'Hadspen Abundance' (rose pink) is a newcomer and is very free flowering. 'Honorine Jobert' (white, single, with green centre surrounded by a ring of orange stamens) is an old favourite.
- *A. nemorosa* (wood anemone). 'Allenii' and 'Robinsoniana' both have star-shaped, lavender-blue flowers. 'Vestal' (white double) and 'Wilks' Giant' (large white single).
- *A. sylvestris* (snowdrop windflower) 'Macrantha' (scented white flowers).

BRIGHT IDEAS

UNUSUAL HOUSEPLANTS

It is possible to grow *A. coronaria* as houseplants and to be rewarded by up to six months of flowers.

Plant up to five tubers in a 20cm/8in pot in good quality, loam-based compost. Keep the compost on the dry side of moist until the plants sprout.

Place plants in a cool (7-16°C/45-60°F), dry and well-ventilated position. Provide plenty of light, although young plants should be protected from full sun.

Water established plants twice weekly; more often in very hot weather. Do not spray the foliage as this will encourage fungal diseases. Once the plants are established, feed every ten days with a liquid feed.

Remove dead flowers at soil level to encourage new buds to form. When flowering is finished and no flower stems are visible, allow the foliage to die back and plant the tubers out in the garden. Do not try to grow the same tubers in a pot the following year; they will only produce weak specimens.

'Honorine Jobert' (above left) exemplifes the classic simplicity of Japanese anemones (A. × hybrida syn A. japonica of gardens).

The wood anemone (A. nemorosa) offers a carpet of foliage set off by star-shaped flowers in spring. The species is white, but 'Robinsoniana' (left) is a pale lavender.

Strong colours are a feature of all A. coronaria varieties. Perhaps the most startling of all is the hot, vivid scarlet of 'Hollandia' syn. 'His Excellency' (above), which positively leaps from the cool green of its deeply divided foliage.

The buttercup-yellow A. ranunculoides (right) thrives in woodland conditions, and grows a little taller than A. nemorosa.

Many excellent garden varieties have been developed from the wild wood anemone (A. nemorosa). One of the best is 'Vestal' (right), a pure white double. All wood anemones hug the ground – few are taller than 15cm/6in – and make a good show in dappled shade.

The Pasque flower (below), once part of the anemone genus, has been reclassified as Pulsatilla vulgaris. It also comes in red, pink and white.

shaped, lavender-blue 'Allenii' and 'Robinsoniana'. 'Vestal' is white and has double flowers; 'Wilks' Giant' (also sold as 'Wilks' White) is larger and single. All wood anemones have a creeping, carpeting habit and grow from rhizomes.

To increase stock, divide the rhizomes when the leaves die back. Blooms appear in spring and early summer and reach a height of about 15cm/6in and a spread of 30cm/12in or more.

A. sylvestris will also thrive in partial or dappled shade. Unlike the wood anemone, however, it likes a well-drained soil. The lovely, delicate white flowers are attractively scented and appear in spring and early summer.

This beauty has a carpeting habit and can be invasive, so pick your site well. Look out for the variety called 'Macrantha', which grows to a height and spread of 30cm/12in.

A. ranunculoides is different from the others in that its spring flowers resemble buttercups and are a deep, rich yellow. It enjoys damp, woodland conditions and has a spreading habit. Height and spread reach 20cm/8in.

A. × lipsiensis, also known as *A. × seemannii*, is a low growing, carpeting variety that enjoys partial shade and good drainage. It grows to about 15cm/6in tall, with a spread of 30cm/12in, and produces a profusion of pale yellow flowers in spring.

WHAT'S IN A NAME?

If you have been searching the catalogues for the Pasque flower (also known as the flower of Easter) under the name of *A. pulsatilla*, you may have been disappointed. It underwent a name change a while back and became *Pulsatilla vulgaris*.

Anemone or not, it is gorgeous and deserves a place in the garden. Its purple or white flowers appear in spring and are followed by seed heads that are lovely in their own right.

Just to confuse you still further, *A. hepatica* is also known as *Hepatica nobilis* and is well worth investigating. It has semi-evergreen, leathery leaves and comes in lilac-mauve, white or pink. It flowers in spring and enjoys damp shady places.

Irises

Versatile and easy to grow, irises make an elegant addition to the flower garden. Plant them around the pond, in borders or in rockeries for year round colour.

Irises form a very large genus of flowering perennials with more than 300 members, most of them ideally suited to gardens. There is, quite literally, an iris for every situation, from a pond, through moist boggy areas to a dry sun-parched border.

By choosing the right varieties you can have irises blooming in every season, their flowers ranging from the purest white, through sunny yellows to the deepest, velvety purple. With some varieties there is the added bonus of a delicious scent, and nearly all types make good cut flowers.

A typical iris is easily recognized by its erect, sword-shaped leaves and distinctive flowers, made up of three inner petals (standards) which usually stand upright, and three larger, outer ones (falls) which fall downwards.

Iris groups

For convenience, commonly-grown garden irises can be split into three main groups, each serving a different purposes in the garden. Bulbous irises include the various border kinds, popular as florists' cut flowers, as well as dwarf, winter and spring alpine species. Water irises grow best in moist soil or shallow water and are ideal for ponds and pools. Bearded irises — so-called because of a line of fleshy hairs on the falls which looks like a beard — are traditionally grown in the herbaceous border and include the

The aptly-named bearded iris, I. pallida 'Bold Print', is remarkable for its striking colour contrasts.

PLANT PROFILE

Suitable site and soil *Iris reticulata* prefers light, well-drained, limy soil; English irises, light moist soil; Dutch irises, light fertile soil, and Spanish irises, light, well-drained soil. Water irises need damp, marshy soil or shallow water, and bearded irises fertile, neutral or slightly alkaline soil. All prefer full sun.

Planting Plant bulbs in early autumn; *I. reticulata* should be 8cm/3in deep, larger bulbs 10-15cm/4-6in deep. Water irises should be planted in early spring or late summer. *I. pseudacorus* should be up to 45cm/18in below water level and *I. laevigata* 15cm/6in deep. Put *I. kaempferi* into damp soil.

Cultivation and care After flowering, *I. reticulata* can be fed once a month for three months with a general liquid fertilizer to ensure good flowers the following year. Do not allow it to get waterlogged. Keep the rhizomes of bearded irises well-watered for the first three weeks and dead-head the flowers in summer.

Propagation Divide bulbs after flowering if required. Divide clumps of rhizomous irises and grow new plants from the offsets. This should be done every three to four years even if you do not want new plants, to ensure continued vigour.

Pests and diseases Generally trouble free, though may suffer aphid attack.

popular 'flag' irises.

The most popular hybrids found in garden centres and bulb catalogues are known as English, Dutch and Spanish irises. English irises derive from *I. latifolia*, Spanish from *I. xiphium*, while the Dutch are hybrids. They have similar, wide ranges of colour.

Given a sunny position in the garden, they are as trouble-free as any of the common spring bulbs, and should be planted in the autumn for a succession of flowers throughout the summer months.

In late winter, I. reticulata (right) can bring vibrant colour to a rockery or window box.

The delightful water iris, I. laevigata alba (far right), flowers in midsummer.

L. laevigata, flanked by Euphorbia griffithii 'Fireglow' (below right), can make a striking display.

The tiny I. danfordiae (below), with glowing yellow flowers, is perfect for a rockery.

Continuous flowers

The Dutch are the first to flower, in early summer, followed in a few weeks by the Spanish and then by the English. By planting a few bulbs of each type, it is possible to have a continuous supply of white, yellow, blue, mauve and purple flowers for cutting, or simply for enjoying in the garden border. The plants will grow to a height of 30-60cm/12-24in.

The Dutch and Spanish irises may not be hardy in some colder areas, and will need

protecting in winter with a cloche. The English irises are the easiest of all to grow, needing no winter protection.

Equally pretty are the dwarf irises, which flower in early spring. They prefer a well-drained soil and make ideal specimens for rockeries and alpine beds, or for growing in pots on the patio; they also make a brave show in a winter window box, where their bright colours are especially welcome in late winter.

I. reticulata grows to just 15cm/6in in height, and produces a delicate, sweetly-scented, blue or purple flower, while *I. danfordiae* is strongly scented and even smaller, just 5-10cm/2-4in tall. The yellow flowers have green spots on the fall petals, while the standards are under-developed; the flowers are rarely as much as 5cm/2in across.

Water lovers

Water irises grow from rhizomes, or fleshy roots, and are best suited to waterside planting. Two species, *Iris kaempferi* and *Iris laevigata*, have beautiful, big flowers, 12-15cm/5-6in across. *I. kaempferi* is happiest in moist soil on

DIVIDE AND RULE

You can increase your stock of irises by dividing up clumps which have become overgrown.

Lift bulbous irises when the foliage has died down (usually in late summer). The bulbs will spilt naturally by hand and once replanted will often flower the following year.

Rhizomes can be divided in the same way. Lift them after flowering, then, using a sharp knife, cut off new pieces from the outside and discard the old centre. Each piece should have one or two strong offshoots. Replant immediately.

GARDEN NOTES

The water iris, I. kaempferi *(left)*, is best planted at the edge of a pond, where its glorious flowers are seen to maximum effect.

The beautiful yellow flag iris, I. pseudacorus *(right)* is another water lover but tends to be invasive in a pond. It grows wild in Britain.

The delicate colours of I. 'Shepherd's Delight' *(below right)* make it a popular border plant and ideal for cut-flower displays.

A favourite border plant, I. 'Jane Phillips' *(far right)* bears delightful pinkish-mauve flowers in early summer.

the edge of the pool, while *I. laevigata* is a true water plant, and ideally likes 15cm/6in of water above the rhizome. Both varieties flower in early to midsummer.

Many water irises originate in Japan – indeed the group is sometimes known as Japanese irises – but *I. sibirica* comes from Siberia. It prefers boggy soil, and grows to 1.2m/4ft, with blue or purple flowers in early summer. Its hybrids, in blue, violet and white, are good garden choices.

The yellow flag iris (*Iris pseudacorus*), with its butter-coloured flowers, grows wild in Britain and is very adaptable, accustoming itself to any water depth up to 46cm/18in. It can reach 1.8m/6ft tall.

Water irises are completely hardy and need no special care. If they start to outgrow the pond, the rhizomes can easily be divided and replanted every three years or so.

Border favourites

The bearded irises also grow from rhizomes, but they are distinguised by a 'beard' of hairs on the downward petals. This group, mainly derived from *I. pallida* and *I. germanica*, contains most of the com-

RECOMMENDED VARIETIES

Dwarf bulbs
I. reticulata 'Harmony'; velvet blue with yellow blaze. 'Violet Beauty'; purple with orange streak. *I. danfordiae*; yellow.

Other bulbs
'White Excelsior'; white Dutch. 'Imperator'; deep blue. 'Golden Emperor'; gold.

Water irises
I. kaempferi; purple, pink, lavender or white marginal or bog plant.
Yellow flag (*I. pseudacorus*); yellow water plant.
I. laevigata; blue or purple marginal. 'Snowdrift' is a pure white double, 'Regal' is red. 'Variegata' has blue flowers and leaves striped with white.

Bearded irises
Purple flag (*I. germanica*); medium-sized rich purple with white beard.
I. pallida 'Bold Print'; medium, white and purple. 'Early Light'; tall, cream and yellow. 'Marhaba'; dwarf blue. 'Mary Frances'; tall, pink to lavender. 'Sable'; tall, with purple petals verging on black. 'Shepherd's Delight'; tall, pale pink.

for the front of the border, where they will form colourful clumps through into the beginning of summer.

The tall ones flower slightly later, and are best grown at the back of the border, where other plants will give them some support. As well as the usual blue, purple and yellow, the colour range includes the pale pink of 'Shepherd's Delight', the lavender of 'Mary Frances' and the unusual golden brown, russet and white shades of 'Flamenco'.

Plant choice

The sheer number of iris varieties can make choosing the right plants for your garden a confusing task. It is really a case of deciding exactly where in the garden you want to grow them and then checking that the conditions are right for each group – moist soil or water for the Japanese irises, a sunny border for bearded and bulbous irises and a rock garden for *Iris reticulata* and the dwarf forms. Having got that right, it is simply a matter of choosing your favourite colours and getting going on the planting.

Iris reticulata bulbs should be planted 8cm/3in deep in a well-drained soil during late summer and early autumn. English, Spanish and Dutch iris bulbs should also be

mon garden hybrids. They are excellent plants for the late spring and early summer herbaceous border, as long as they have plenty of sun. Heights vary from the tiniest dwarf varieties, measuring only 10cm/4in, to the majestic tall forms which reach heights of up to 1.5m/5ft.

The spring-flowering dwarf irises, including the deep blue 'Marhaba', are best suited to rockeries where the drainage is good, while the medium-sized ones, such as 'Bold Print', whose white petals are edged with purple, are ideal

planted at this time, at a depth of 10-15cm/4-6in.

Water irises can be planted in either spring or autumn on the margins of the pond, while the rhizomes of bearded irises can be planted at the beginning or end of the summer.

The top of the rhizome should be just visible above the surface of the soil and it is important to keep them moist for the first few weeks after planting has been done.

Once established, all irises are easy to care for. They do not need attention or special watering or feeding. However, the taller varieties will benefit from staking with a bamboo cane during their first year of growth. If, after three or four years, the clumps have outgrown their allotted space, or if the flowers are poor, it is a simple task to divide them up to create new plants.

Poppies

**right, beautiful poppies create vibrant,
e-catching colour and bring a lively touch
to both town and country gardens.**

erhaps one of the most evocative of all flowers, .e poppy *(Papaver)* capti- ates the heart and eye of even he most reluctant of garden- ers. The romantics may pic- ture country fields of swaying corn flushed red with hue of fragile wild poppies. The more stylistically inclined may im- agine an oriental extravagan- za of bold colours and textures. Whichever type you are, there is a poppy to suit you and your garden, whether in the town or country, formal or informal.

Bursting with colour

The range of richly coloured poppies is wide and includes many hardy annuals, a few biennials and some herba- ceous perennials.

Introduce poppies which will complement your garden features. If you have a rock garden, try nestling a few al- pine poppies against a large rock. The green-grey leaves are surmounted by flowers in white, yellow, red and orange and make a stunning contrast with the stark rocks.

Rockery poppies

A thin layer of shingle over the compost in the rockery creates further interest. It contrasts with both the flowers and deeply notched leaves, as well as preventing soil splashing on them during heavy rain.

The vibrancy of colour in a border of hardy annuals can be further enhanced by the field poppy, a hardy annual with richly coloured flowers. Keep the patches relatively small,

Of all field poppies, the variety Papaver rhoeas 'Shirley Single Mixed' (above) is the most popular. It is perfect for any wild-flower garden. Borne on slender stems, the petals look as if they are painted in watercolours, the delicate shades intensifying towards the edges.

The oriental poppy, P. orientale 'Diana' (left), has a flower so exquisite it seems to have been made from tissue paper. Set on a tall, thick stem the rich pink petals are blotched with black at the base.

as they can soon overwhelm less colourful flowers.

The oriental poppy is best suited to permanent borders and especially those with a rustic aura. These plants have a slightly sprawling nature that enables them to harmon- ize easily with old brick paths and walls.

Floppy poppies

Towards the end of the sum- mer clumps of oriental poppy can become rather unsightly. They are therefore best planted with other plants in front of them to hide their sprawling and flopping

PLANT PROFILE

Suitable site and soil: a well-drained, relatively light soil and a position in full sun are essential. Avoid cold, wet soils and heavy shade.

Cultivation and care: remove dead flower heads of hardy annual and biennial poppies to prevent seeds falling and germinating. With herbaceous perennial types, also remove faded flowers. This ensures that the plant's energies are directed into growth rather than the formation of seeds. Use pea-sticks to support plants, inserting them early in the season so that shoots grow up and through them. Allow herbaceous perennials to die down naturally in autumn, then tidy up by removing dead stems and leaves. Once hardy annuals and biennials have flowered, dig up and discard in autumn.

Propagation: sow hardy annual seeds 6mm/¼in deep from March to May in the positions in which they are to grow and flower. Germination takes 10-14 days. When the seedlings are large enough to handle thin them 20-30cm/8-12in apart. Biennial types are sown 6mm/¼in deep in light soil in May or June, in their flowering positions. In autumn thin out seedlings to 30-38cm/12-15in apart.

They can also be sown in a seed-bed and transplanted in autumn into their flowering positions. Take care not to damage roots.

Sow seeds of herbaceous perennial types 6mm/¼in deep from June to August. When the seedlings are large enough to handle thin them to 15cm/6in apart. In mild areas move the young plants into their flowering positions in October or November: set those of the oriental poppy 45-60cm/1½-2ft apart. In cold regions, wait until March or April to transplant them.

Herbaceous perennials can also be increased by lifting and dividing congested plants in March or April and replanting young parts from around the outside of the clump. Discard woody parts from the centre of the old plant and replant the young parts to the same depth. Increase oriental poppies by root cuttings from autumn to late winter during the plant's dormant season.

Pests and diseases: downy mildew may create yellow blotches on leaves. Dust or spray with a fungicide.

PICK A POPPY

Iceland poppies create stunning arrangements indoors. For a long-lasting display cut them when the buds are just showing colour. Immediately scald the cut stem ends in boiling water to seal them. The capsule-like heads of the oriental poppy are eye-catching when dried and displayed indoors during winter. Arrange these with other dried flowers to make an attractive, everlasting centrepiece.

The Iceland poppy, P. nudicaule (right) is a tuft forming, short-lived perennial which is best grown as a biennial. Between June and July few flowers can compete with this delicately fragranced, bright-faced gem. Ideal for rock gardens, these poppies come in a wide range of colours which will enliven the stark background. This variety is called 'Summer Breeze' and is vibrant orange with a splash of yellow in the centre. A slightly shaded environment will ensure the Iceland poppy thrives.

2in wide. They are available in white and many shades of yellow, orange and red. This is a short-lived perennial which is best raised as a biennial.

Another short-lived perennial is the Iceland poppy *(P. nudicaule)*. During June and July few other plants can compete with its slightly fragrant, 6.5cm/2½in wide, bright-faced, paper-textured flowers in a

There are no prizes for guessing why these stunning red and black poppies (above) got their names. The variety is called 'Lady Bird' and it belongs to the species P. commutatum. The flowers are up to 6.5cm/2½ in wide and appear in June to August on slender, elegant stems which are 45cm/18in tall. The striking markings are in fact there for a purpose. They are called honey guides and help bees find their way to the nectar in the centre.

nature. The opium poppy also has country garden charm, with large flowers atop elegant, long stems.

Going wild!

Wild and natural gardens can be enriched with poppies, as well as by many other native British plants. Many seed companies sell field poppies in individual packets, as well as in mixtures with other native flowers such as primroses, cowslips, field scabious, foxgloves, wild pansies, cornflowers and corn marigolds.

Most gardens have a bright and sunny spot which is ideal for a wild flower garden. Within a few months it can be bursting with colour. If you already have field poppies or opium poppies in other parts of your garden, collect the seedheads and, when ripe, scatter the seeds in this area.

Some perennial poppies

GARDEN NOTES

POPPY IMPOSTERS

Not all poppies are poppies! Many plants have misleading common names:

- Welsh poppy *(Meconopsis cambrica)*
- poppy tree *(Romneya)*
- plume poppy *(Macleaya)*
- prickly poppy *(Argemone mexicana)*
- Californian poppy *(Eschscholzia californica)*
- Himalayan blue poppy *(Meconopsis betonicifolia)*

tend to be so short-lived that invariably they are better sown, then raised as biennials.

The alpine poppy *(P. alpinum)* is superb in a rock garden, creating a dazzling summer display of flowers up to 5cm/

wide colour range. Plants vary in height, from 45-60cm/1½-2ft and in width, from 30-45cm/12-18in. Varieties now include a wide range of glorious colours including white, yellow, orange, pink, salmon and rose, as well as some fancy-edged types.

P. commutatum, also known as *P. rhoeas commutatum*, is a hardy annual with vividly

The notorious opium poppy (below) is swathed in an aura of oriental mystique. Standing tall on greyish-green stems 75-90cm/2½-3ft high they are ideal for the back of a border. The crimson petals are ragged delicately at the edge, and the underside is a beautifully contrasting shade of pale pink.

coloured flowers up to 6.5cm/2½in wide from June to August. Invariably it is the stunningly attractive variety 'Lady Bird' that is grown. It is so called because it has red flowers which have a black blotch in the centre – just like the markings of a ladybird.

The oriental poppy is one of the most eye-catching of all herbaceous perennials. Bright

scarlet flowers up to 10cm/4in wide are borne from May to June amid deeply indented, hairy leaves. As well as the scarlet flowers, there are many superb varieties in pretty colours including pink, white and orange.

The field poppy *(P. rhoeas)* is a hardy annual, familiar for its decoration of cornfields from June to August with its very

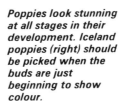

Poppies look stunning at all stages in their development. Iceland poppies (right) should be picked when the buds are just beginning to show colour.

The fluffy double-flowered opium poppy, P. somniferum 'Pink Chiffon' (below), displays all the stages of its development: the hairy green sepals open to reveal delicate pink petals, which in turn expose the seed head when the petals drop off.

bright scarlet flowers with black centres. In gardens it is equally attractive, with flowers up to 7.5cm/3in wide in an extensive colour range and borne on stems up to 60cm/2ft high from clumps 25-30cm/10-12in wide. The well-known Shirley Poppies are derived from the field poppy in a range of colours.

Another popular species for flower borders is the opium poppy *(P. somniferum)*. This is a well-known hardy annual with dominant 10cm/4in wide flowers through the summer on plants 75-90cm/2½-3ft high and 30-38cm/12-15in wide.

Clever combinations

Plant poppies alongside other plants to produce a whole host of stunning effects. The rich colours of the field poppy create an attractive contrast in colour and shape with the narrow, mid-green and arching leaves of the feather grass *(Stipa pennata)*. The silvery-buff plumes of this ornamental grass will arch and mingle with the poppy flowers.

Oriental poppies, border irises and clarkia *(Clarkia elegans)* together create a long season of colour. The clarkia is wispy enough to be planted

SPECIES AND VARIETIES

- Alpine poppy *(P. alpinum)* in a range of colours.
- 'Lady Bird' *(P. commatatum),* looks like its namesake, red with black blotches.
- Iceland poppy *(P. nudicaule):* 'Garden Gnome Mixed', with flowers in scarlet, yellow, salmon, orange, yellow and white, or 'Oregon Rainbows' in a wide colour range, apricot and peach, pink, lavender-rose, white-green with cream, pink and lemon.
- Oriental poppy *(P. orientale):* 'Black and White', has white flowers with black centres. 'Blue Moon' is mauve-pink with black throat markings and maroon veins, the petals

of 'Curlilocks' are ruffled orange-red, 'Mrs Perry' is salmon pink, 'Picotee' has a frilled salmon edge on a white base and 'Turkish Delight' is flesh-pink.
- Field poppy *(P. rhoeas):* 'Rev. Wilkes Mixed', semi-double and single-flowered blooms in many colours. 'Shirley Re-selected Double Mixed', in shades of white, pink, rose, crimson and salmon, and 'Mother of Pearl' in pastels.
- Opium poppy *(P. somniferum).* 'Paeony Flowered Mixed', large, double flowers in a wide colour range and 'Paeony Flowered Pink Beauty', double, salmon-pink flowers.

The alpine poppy (above) will nestle in a rock garden or grow happily by a wall. It forms tufts of grey-green deeply serrated leaves from which elegant leafless stems arise. They grow to a height of 20cm/8in, raising their sunny yellow faces to the sky.

The seed heads of the opium poppy, P. somniferum (right), are most suitable for drying. They make beautiful additions to dried-flower arrangements but are unusual enough to be displayed on their own. Cut the long stems of the seed heads and hang them upside down in a well-aerated, warm place until they are a bluish-grey shade.

amid early and mid-season flowering perennials, where it continues the display into late summer or early autumn. The oriental poppy also creates a colour and shape contrast with the stiffly upright and grass-like gardener's garters (*Phalaris arundinacea* 'Picta'). The white-striped leaves of the grass contrasts with the up-turned, vividly coloured and dark-centred poppies.

Soft-coloured varieties of oriental poppies can be used with other pastel-coloured flowers to create an underplanting for pink, peach and buff-coloured roses. Avoid using strongly coloured poppies, as they will soon dominate the roses.

BEAUTIFUL BUT DANGEROUS

The fruits (seed-heads) and the sap of the opium poppy are poisonous, while all parts of the Iceland poppy are said to be poisonous. The field poppy is dangerous to animals if eaten in large amounts. If in doubt about your safety, wear gloves when handling poppies and certainly do not chew them!

DON'T FORGET!

PERFECT PARTNERS COLOUR CONTRASTS

A tall-growing opium poppy has been grown with Lavatera olbia 'Rosea', commonly known as tree mallow (left). Both plants flower through the summer. The slender poppy stems bear just one flower with a stunning yellow centre, making an interesting contrast with clusters of mallow flowers.

Poppies are at their most spectacular when growing wild in a cornfield (below). The bright scarlet flowers with black centres of the field poppy, P. rhoeas, add vibrant colour to the rural landscape in the middle of summer. Cornflowers provide a glorious touch of blue and mayweed a hint of white. Why not copy this effect by designating an area of your garden for wild flowers?

Lilacs

The showy blooms produced by garden lilacs, and their heady fragrance, make them as popular today as when they were introduced at the turn of the century.

It is no wonder that lilac is many people's favourite shrub. The flowers are spectacular, borne in large spikes or panicles and coming in a host of subtle colours. As the name suggests, these are mainly in shades of lavender, violet and purple, but there are also deep red, pale yellow and blue lilacs, and beautiful pure white ones. What is more, they all have a really strong and utterly delightful fragrance, and are good for cutting.

Such treasures are often fussy, hard-to-grow plants, but not the lilac. It is very hardy, and will flourish in any reasonably well drained soil; nor is it particular as to the amount of sun or shade it gets. The opulent flowers will appear in abundance, year after year, without having the benefit of expert annual pruning.

If lilac has a fault it is that it can be over-enthusiastic – the common lilac can throw out a lot of suckers, and grow into a tree too big for a small garden – but that is a problem easily remedied by picking a less vigorous variety, or a dwarf one.

Spoilt for choice

The large lilac family contains a number of different species and hybrids, but the most popular plants are the innumerable garden lilacs – varieties of the common lilac, *Syringa vulgaris*. This is said to be the parent of more hybrids than any other shrub – more than 500, though only a small proportion of them are commercially available.

Most of them grow to around

3.5m/12ft tall, and almost as broad. The difference between them is almost entirely in the colour of the flowers, and whether these are single or double. The leaves are also attractive, generally large and heart-shaped, with a fresh-looking, light green colour. Flowering time comes early,

from mid-spring to early summer, according to variety.

Catalogues often categorize lilacs according to whether they are double or single flowered. But, as the individual florets are tiny, achieving their spectacular effect by being thickly massed on the spike, it does not make much

PLANT PROFILE

Suitable site and soil Any fertile, well-drained soil, though one with a high lime content is ideal. Full sun is preferable, but semi-shade acceptable.
Planting Dress liberally with bone meal.
Cultivation and care Annual pruning is not essential for flowering, but stops the bush getting straggly and leggy. As soon as growth starts in spring cut back new plants to a pair of buds to make them bushy – growth comes from the tips of the shoots only. Once established, just cut out all weak and straggly growth after flowering, thin out old wood occasionally and trim to shape if needed. Also remove dead flower spikes before they set seed. Pull off any suckers just below ground level – if pruned off they multiply. Give a dressing of decayed manure, compost or bone meal every spring. Alternatively, mulch with leaves in autumn. If soil is not chalky, dress with lime every few years.
Propagation Lilacs are easy to increase by taking semi-ripe or hardwood cuttings or by layering branches that grow near the ground. Suckers can also be planted, but are likely to turn out different from the parent – many are grafted on common lilac rootstocks, some on privet.
Pests and diseases Lilacs can be prone to bacterial blight that blackens their leaves. Cut out and destroy all affected parts.

Lilacs have given their name to a colour, but the ingenuity of the hybridizer has widened the plant's range considerably from the species, S. vulgaris (left). 'Massena' (above) has darkened the basic colour to purple-red, while the double-flowered 'Madame Lemoine' (below) is white. The wine red 'Souvenir de Louis Spaeth' (right) was one of the earliest hybrids developed.

difference to the overall look of the plant.

Double-flowered varieties have a slightly lusher look, but some people prefer the single-flowered types, as the form of the individual florets is easier to see. Both double and single are equally fragrant.

The subtle colour variations of lilac blossom are hard to pin down in words. The same variety may be described quite differently by two different nurseries. Apart from the fact that the difference between the flower colour of many hybrids is not very great, the colour of the spike often changes depending on whether it is composed of buds. Besides, a young lilac bush may not develop its true colour for several seasons. The thing to look for is the intensity of the colour – decide whether you want flowers that are pale and delicate, or rich and dark.

Garden lilacs

Many garden lilacs were raised in France at the turn of the century by Victor and Emile Lemoine, and many of these – such as 'Madame Lemoine' – are as popular as ever today. They are all varieties and hybrids springing from *Syringa vulgaris;* the ones crossed with *S. oblata* (predominatly blue) are sometimes listed as *S. hyacinthiflora.*

The early varieties have now been joined by a great many new ones, many of which are not noticeably different from one another. The average garden centre will only stock a selection of the best ones, reliably hardy and with large flower spikes.

Two long-time favourites are both white – 'Madame Lemoine', which has double flowers, and 'Maud Notcutt',

which is single, 'Vestale' is another long-established, single-flowered white.

Good varieties in the classic lilac colour range with single flowers include 'Esther Staley' (almost pink), 'Massena' (deep red-purple) and 'Clarke's Giant' (rosy-mauve to lilac blue – good for allowing to develop into a small tree).

One of the oldest of all lilacs, 'Souvenir de Louis Spaeth', with deep wine-red flowers, has always been extremely popular, as it has a reputation for being consistent and reliable. Another excellent deep-coloured one is 'Congo', with dark lilac-red spikes.

Notable among those with double flowers are 'Charles Joly' (deep purple-red, fading with age), 'Katherine Havemeyer' (purple-lavender fading to pink), 'Madame Antoine Buchner' (rosy mauve) and Mrs Edward Harding (claret-red, shaded with pink).

If you want a truly blue lilac, look for 'Blue Hyacinth' (mauve in bud, single flowers appearing as early as the end of April). The yellow one is easy to spot – it's called 'Primrose'. For something rather

The pale yellow colouring of the flowers of 'Primrose' (left) is unique among lilacs.

'Blue Hyacinth' (left below) is sometimes a true, pale blue, but more often, as here, has a mauve tint.

'Madame Antoine Buchner' has double flowers, but this is only apparent when the flower clusters are seen from close up (right). From even a short distance away, the individual flowers dissolve into a mass of colour.

While most S. vulgaris varieties eventually make fairly large shrubs, S. microphylla (below) is perfectly at home in a medium-sized shrub border, where it will produce a profusion of highly-scented pink panicles in early to midsummer.

GARDEN NOTES

NOT LILAC AT ALL

The Latin name of the lilac genus, *Syringa*, can cause confusion with a completely different shrub often commonly known as syringa, or mock orange. This is properly *Philadelphus*, which has larger flowers, always white, borne in clusters instead of spikes. It has an even stronger, blossomy scent than lilac.

unusual, look for 'Sensation', which is purple-red edged with white, though it can revert and lose the variegation.

Variations on a theme

With one or two exceptions, species lilacs are less widely stocked in garden centres, as the large-flowered garden varieties are more popular. For a really tiny garden, *Syringa microphylla* is an ideal choice, as it is much smaller than most, reaching no more than

The two-tone colouring of 'Sensation' produces an attractive effect both close-up (left) and at a distance, but unfortunately the plant sometimes loses this characteristic, with the flowers reverting to plain purple.

The lovely red flowers of 'Mrs Edward Harding' (below) appear a little later than those of other hybrids.

about 1.8m/6ft high and wide. Naturally the flower spikes are also smaller – but there should be a compensatory second flush in autumn. The flower colour is pink-purple, or rose-pink in the variety 'Superba', which continues to flower intermittently right through to mid-autumn.

Another fairly small one, growing about 2.1m/7ft each way, is the charming Persian lilac (*S. × persica*), with a neat rounded shape, long narrow leaves and small, but delightfully abundant, lilac or white flowers.

For something distinctly different, and not too large, look for the cut-leaved lilac, *S. × persica* 'Laciniata'. This has an open, graceful habit of growth, and dissected, featherylooking leaves. Flowers are violet-purple.

About the same size, and guaranteed super-hardy, is the Rouen or Chinese lilac, *S. × chinensis,* a hybrid between *S. laciniata* and *S. vulgaris* that reaches 3m/10ft high and 2.1m/7ft across. This has lilacpurple flowers (reddish-lilac in the variety 'Saugeana'). Also very hardy are the many varieties developed from *S. × josiflexa*. These are bigger shrubs, 3.5m/12ft high and wide. 'Bellicent' (clear pink) is a popular variety.

Buying lilacs

Choose your lilac carefully, especially if your garden is small – pick one of the less vigorous varieties, or the miniature *S. microphylla*. To get the colour you want, do not rely on catalogue or garden centre descriptions, or colour photographs. If at all possible, see the plant in flower before you buy. Even that may not be a reliable guide, as lilac colours are so changeable! But why worry – all lilacs are beautiful.

Lovely Lavender

Easy to grow, evergreen and adaptable, lavender is an all-time favourite and its delightful scent will enhance any garden.

Probably the first thing that comes to mind when you think of lavender is its scent. For centuries its evocative perfume has graced all kinds of gardens from humble cottages to stately homes.

There are many varieties of lavender. Traditionally, there were three main types – English, French and Dutch – and five main varieties have now been developed which encompass all the best qualities these old plants had to offer, with the added bonus of resistance to disease.

Winter interest

Winter can be a dreary time in the garden with very little colour or interest. Use the light-colour evergreen foliage of a range of lavender varieties to provide contrast with other plants. The foliage of lavender varies according to the type you decide on. Most have silvery green leaves, but some have a more vivid green colour, which provides a welcome contrast to the dark foliage of many evergreens.

Easy to grow

If you are one of those busy people who has little time or energy to devote to the garden, you will be pleased to know that lavender needs the minimum of attention.

It is a hardy perennial which means that, once planted, it can more or less be left to its own devices. Light pruning helps it to keep a good

Lavandula angustifolia 'Hidcote' (right) is colourful and aromatic. Lavender attracts butterflies, like the common blue (inset).

99

shape and encourages it to flower happily year after year.

Bees and butterflies

Lavender is an environmentally friendly plant, attracting a wide range of insects, especially butterflies and bees. Bees are highly desirable allies for any gardener as their pollen-gathering activities ensure that plants are fertilized and produce seeds.

The benefits of insect pollinators are obvious when growing peas or beans, for example, as it is the seeds of these plants that we eat. Lots of insects in the garden mean plenty of peas and beans to eat. So it makes sense to plant lavender near vegetables to attract these benefactors.

Bees and other insects are also the friends of the busy flower gardener and encourage self-seeding of annuals and biennials. The insects that lavender will attract to your beds and borders will encourage such self-seeding plants as foxgloves and hollyhocks. Not only do you save money by not having to buy so many seeds, it is the easiest way of increasing your plants. All you need to do is transplant seedlings to other parts of the garden.

Shapes and design

Lavender is very useful if you want to create interesting shaped beds outlined by a low hedge. Because it is an evergreen, lavender ensures that your design keeps its shape throughout the winter. If cut back at the end of every growing season, it will stay compact and neat for years.

Ideal for a purple or pink border, this unusual French lavender, L. stoechas pedunculata (above) has deep purple flowers topped by lighter coloured plume-like bracts, from late spring.

The lavender variety 'Jean Davis' (right) has exquisitely pale flowers, perfect for a pale pink or white border and equally at home in town or country gardens.

L. angustifolia 'Nana Alba' (right) is a popular dwarf, compact lavender, with pretty white flowers. Growing to a height of only 30cm, its leaves are broader than many other varieties. Placed towards the front of a border, it will harmonize particularly well with blue and purple flowers, or with white-flowered plants.

'Loddon Pink' is a compact form of lavender, growing to about 60-75cm high. The very pale pink flowers look beautiful against a background of green such as this well-kept hedge and lawn (right).

When planting in a rock garden or at the front of a small bed or border, choose low-growing 'Dwarf Munstead' (below). It has all the characteristics of the classic lavender – blue-purple flower spikes, grey-green leaves and a delightful fragrance – but in a compact form.

LAVENDER AND LACE

Use your sewing skills to create pretty sachets, or weave stems with ribbon to make a lavender 'dolly'.

For a lavender 'dolly', tie strong thread tightly around a fresh bunch of lavender, just below flower heads. Bend stalks over to enclose flowers and weave with ribbon.

To dry lavender, pick soon after the flower spikes appear, tie in bunches and hang upside down in a dark, airy place. Use in dried flower arrangements or in lavender bags or pot pourri.

In a garden with a neat, formal design, some lavenders are suitable for growing as fragrant, low hedges in place of the more traditional box.

Besides being a great asset in such places as beds, borders, the vegetable patch and the herb garden, lavender can also be used in its dwarf form in a rockery. There is a dwarf white variety (*L. stoechas* 'Alba') which is particularly valuable for this.

You can grow all types of lavender in containers as long as you cut them back at the end of the flowering season to ensure they do not get too straggly. What could be more delightful at the end of a long, hard day than sitting on the patio, surrounded by that heavenly scent and the soothing hum of bees?

Buying lavender
When shopping for lavender plants, first decide how you are going to use them.

If you have a large garden and want an informal hedge, 'Royal Purple' would be a good choice. The body of the plant reaches a height of 45–60cm/ 18–24in and the flower spikes rise above this. Its deep purple flowers appear in the height of

ple flowers. 'Alba' is a white variety. Neither is fully hardy so they are suitable only for milder areas.

Planting and caring

You can plant container-grown lavender at any time. Bare-rooted plants, on the other hand, should be planted out in early spring or autumn. They enjoy full sun but will tolerate some shade.

Lavenders will adapt to most soils so it is not necessary to go to great lengths in preparing the ground. They do like a well-drained spot, though, so do not plant in boggy places. Heavy clay soil may need some help to improve drainage.

These plants do not need

summer and are very fragrant and particularly favoured for drying.

Another good hedging type is 'Loddon Pink'. This grows to 60cm/24in and has vivid green leaves. The flowers appear continuously throughout the summer months.

If you are planning an ornamental herb or vegetable plot then you will need a low hedging variety such as *L. angustifolia* 'Hidcote', 'Imperial Gem' or 'Princess Blue'.

'Hidcote' grows to about 45cm/18in and has deep violet flowers. The foliage is grey and downy. 'Imperial Gem' is very similar and both flower during the summer.

The 'Princess Blue' variety has true lavender blue flowers and silvery foliage. This variety flowers in early summer.

L. stoechas (French lavender) does well in rockeries or as an edging plant for flower beds. It grows to 30cm/12ins and has very deep pur-

'Hidcote' (above) is one of the best and most popular lavender varieties. Its dense spikes of violet flowers look lovely highlighted with splashes of bright yellow in a shrub border. The santolina in this border is an ideal partner plant, as is the rosemary. All three plants produce their own distinctive fragrances which mingle deliciously.

Lavender is very much at home in a cottage garden, alongside such plants as foxgloves, cornflowers and delphiniums. Here (left) the daisy-like Agyranthemum 'Jamaica Primrose' and rose campion (Lychnis coronaria) give a cottagey feel to a town garden.

The lavender-blue flowers of L. angustifolia 'Munstead' create a bold splash and harmonize perfectly with other blue flowers, or with white or yellow as in this garden (right). Why not plant this variety as ground cover at the front of a large border, or as a low hedge to surround a herb garden?

much feeding. In fact, if you over-feed lavender, it is inclined to produce too much foliage at the expense of flowers.

Lavender is a shrubby plant and therefore needs pruning if it is not to get too straggly. Simply cut back to the end of the green stems when flowering is over.

Plant partners

Lavender is a good mixer and goes well with virtually anything. The dwarf varieties will settle down happily with any plants to be found in a rock garden, such as alpines.

Many people use the edging varieties of lavender to outline their rose beds. This is particularly successful if you choose the colours of both roses and

A lavender hedge bordering a front path (above) not only looks attractive, but smells heavenly as you brush past it. Here, the front door of the house, painted a soft grey-green, matches the foliage, helping to create a peaceful atmosphere.

L. angustifolia 'Hidcote' makes a particularly good hedge. The flowers, though not particularly fragrant, are deep blue-purple. This variety has a naturally neat habit but will require trimming twice a year, in late summer and in spring.

lavenders carefully. For instance, plant pale pink roses with light blue lavender, or yellow roses with dark purple lavender. The foliage of both plants makes a pleasing combination too.

No herb garden would be complete without lavender. The scent attracts pollinators and this in turn encourages some of your herbs to self seed. Low hedging varieties of lavender make an attractive and fragrant boundary.

Lavender makes a delightful foil for the more flamboyant summer bedding plants. Containers and beds packed full of bright annuals will benefit from the addition of its sta-

LOVELY LAVENDER RECIPES

The lavender flower is edible, and may be candied or added to icing for decorating cakes or biscuits.

Lavender vinegar is simple to make and will add an interesting new flavour to your usual salad dressing. Just add a few flower heads to a bottle of white wine vinegar and allow it to steep for a few weeks before use. Lavender oil can be made in much the same way, using a light oil such as sunflower as a base.

Add flowers to your bath or put them in a bottle of distilled water to make a perfumed facial rinse. Strain through a sieve before use so that you are just left with perfumed water. Store in a small bottle sealed with a cork.

BRIGHT IDEAS

tely spikes and gentle foliage.

The enduring popularity of lavender over the centuries is a tribute to its many fine qualities. It is very attractive all year-round, easy to grow, and bushes out rapidly for quick results. It has medicinal properties as well as culinary uses. You can dry the flowers and use them to perfume your home in lavender bags and pot pourri or use them to flavour vinegar. Lavender even repels moths! No wonder it is such a long-lasting favourite.

Dahlias

Dahlias offer you dazzling colour all summer and into autumn, along with plenty of cut flowers – all with the minimum of care.

You could not choose more worthwhile plants than dahlias and, what is more, you do not even need a garden to grow them – dwarf varieties are ideally suited to tubs or window boxes on a balcony.

Dahlias are perennials, capable of living for a number of years, but they are tender, so cannot be left outdoors over winter. The first frosts of autumn will blacken and kill the leaves and stems. The plants form large fleshy tubers, which allow them to have a long rest over winter as they store food and water.

Dahlias are split into two groups: the dwarf kinds which can be used for mass planting or formal summer bedding, as well as for tubs and window boxes, and the tall border varieties. The dwarf varieties grow 30-60cm/1-2ft high and border dahlias reach an average height of 90-120cm/3-4ft.

The flowers, especially those of the taller dahlias, vary greatly in shape. Dwarf bedding types have either single blooms, with a ring of petals, or double, with many petals forming a ball shape.

Tall dahlias

The most popular groups among the tall dahlias include decorative flowered, which have double flowers formed of broad flat petals; cactus-flowered, with double spiky flowers; and semi-cactus-flowered, midway between the

Decorative dahlias, whose broad, flat petals tend to curve in slightly at the edges, are available in a dazzling range of colours (above), though there is no blue. Many of the double flowers are multi-coloured, such as 'Master Robert' (above, inset).

two. Flower size in each group ranges from miniature to giant.

Other popular forms include water-lily-flowered, where the blooms look like water-lilies; collerette, single flowers which have a central collar of contrasting petals; ball dahlias with blooms the size of tennis balls; and pompon dahlias, with golf-ball-sized flowers.

Dahlias come in almost every colour you can imagine. There are all shades of red, pink, orange, yellow, purple and white. Some varieties are bi-coloured, consisting of two contrasting colours; others have several colours blending into each other. In many dahlias the colours are brilliant and dazzling, but others come in quieter pastel shades.

Dahlias are divided into groups according to the size and type of their flower heads and, in fact, the shapes of dahlia flowers are almost as varied as their colours. Cactus-flowered varieties (above) have a shock of long, thin petals. Semi-cactus varieties have flowers of similar shape although the petals are slightly wider.

Collerette dahlias, such as 'La Cierva' (left), are single-flowered with an inner ring, often of another colour (as in this example). They typically display dramatic – some may say – melodramatic – colour contrasts. Collerette dahlias usually have strong stems, so they are particularly good for flower arrangements.

Compact ball dahlias such as 'Wootton Cupid' (right) have densely packed, almost tubular petals. This popular variety reaches a height of about 90-120cm/3-4ft with flowers 8-10cm/ 3-4in across and is a favourite exhibition dahlia. Pompon dahlias bear a close resemblance to ball varieties but are much smaller, being only about 5cm/2in across.

There are various ways of buying dahlias. Undoubtedly the easiest is to purchase dormant tubers in winter or spring from a garden centre, supermarket or mail order dahlia specialist. Young plants can be bought in spring from garden centres or specialists, but these may be inconvenient for some people as they cannot be planted out until all danger of frost is over; in the meantime they must be kept in a light, frost-proof place such as a heated greenhouse. You could also raise your own bedding dahlias from seeds.

Dahlias are fussy about growing conditions, but if

Dahlia enthusiasts tend to grow taller varieties in special beds; they can, however, look very well at the back of a mixed border (left), where their dense foliage provides a backdrop for smaller plants and their blooms add a crowning splash of colour. Tall dahlias do, however, need to be staked, as here, to support the stems as they grow.

PLANTS GREW POORLY

Q Last year I grew some dahlias for the first time. The weather was very hot but growth was very poor and stunted. What was the cause?

A It is very likely that your plants suffered from water shortage. Dahlias need lots of water in the growing season. Always keep the soil moist.

these are right they are very easy plants to grow. Full sun is absolutely essential for strong growth and prolific flowering. In partial or full shade growth will be weak and spindly and few flowers will be produced.

Soil types

Most soil types are suitable for dahlias provided they are well drained – if they stay extremely wet, or pools of water lie on the surface after rain, the plants are liable to rot. The soil needs to be able to hold on to moisture during dry periods though, as dahlias are thirsty plants. In very dry soil conditions, growth will be stunted and flowering reduced.

The best way to prepare the ground for dahlias is to dig in plenty of peat, peat substitute such as coconut fibre, or garden compost before planting.

Containers such as tubs and window boxes should be filled with a soil-less potting compost, either peat-based or one of the new coconut-fibre composts. Dahlias are also greedy feeders, so before planting apply a flower garden fertilizer according to the instructions on the pack.

If all you want is masses of

The single-flowered 'Coltness Hybrids' (below) are dwarf varieties with lobed leaves and daisy-like flowers. Though perennial like all dahlias, they are often grown as annuals.

colour in the garden without much work, there is no doubt that dwarf dahlias are your best bet. They are also the first choice for containers.

Tall dahlias are best for cutting but they need more time spent on cultivation as they must be provided with supports to which the stems are tied as they grow. The best

REMOVING BUDS

The largest possible flowers are obtained by removing some of the flower buds, particularly useful if you want cut flowers or blooms for showing.

Each stem carries a central flower bud at the top with two more buds below it. If a large bloom is required pinch out the lower buds, leaving the central one.

supports for dahlias are the 2.5cm/1in square wooden dahlia stakes that are available from garden centres. Alternatively, you could use very thick bamboo canes. Before buying stakes, it is best to find out the final height of the particular variety of dahlia. You can then choose a stake that is a little bit shorter than the plant after being inserted 30cm/12in into the ground, so that is does not tower above it in an unsightly way. The stakes, one for each plant, should be inserted before planting the tubers or young plants.

As the stems grow, loosely tie in each one to the stake with soft green garden string, making a figure-of-eight loop around stake and stem.

Plant combinations

In the garden dahlias can be effectively combined with various other plants. It is important to grow them only with plants that need the same conditions.

These days many people grow all their plants in mixed borders of shrubs, perennials, bulbs and annuals. Dahlias can be included, too, with tall varieties in the centre or back, and dwarf forms at the front.

Dahlias look superb mixed with shrubs noted for autumn leaf colour or berries, such as cotinus, rhus, cotoneaster, euonymus and berberis. The basically rounded or ball-shaped blooms of dahlias also contrast strikingly with hardy perennials that have spikes of flowers, such as delphiniums.

Dwarf bedding dahlias can be combined with other summer bedding plants. There are many combinations but an idea that works well is to have foliage plants like the silver-leaved *Senecio bicolor cineraria* (usually sold as *Cineraria maritima*) dotted among massed dahlias.

Dahlias can be used as a focus in the creation of a sub-tropical bedding scheme. For example, the main planting can consist of dwarf bedding dahlias. Among these plant varieties of canna (Indian shot) and tender fuchsias, whose delicate colours and pendulous flower forms provide a delightful contrast.

'Doris Day' (below), a tall cactus-flowered dahlia with relatively small blooms, is one of the most richly-coloured red varieties available.

Nasturtiums

Nasturtiums are old favourites in cottage gardens. Although mostly used as bedding plants, they will also climb, trail or add spice to your salad.

Nasturtiums are homely plants that most people like to have around because they are cosy and familiar. Bright, cheerful and easy going, their very lack of temperament has meant they have attracted little in the way of keen interest from most competitive growers.

Fuchsias, delphiniums and others can become an obsession and have whole books dedicated to describing their likes and dislikes, but the obliging nasturtium usually warrants a mere few lines at best. However, there is far more interest to these humble charmers than this lack of attention would suggest.

A place in history

Nasturtiums were well known in Elizabethan England. Their peppery leaves and attractive flowers were much prized as an ingredient of salads. In fact, the name 'Nasturtium' rightly belongs to that other peppery character, watercress. The confusion arose as the newcomer from the West Indies came to be known as 'Indian Cress.' The plant's correct botanical name is *Tropaeolum majus*.

Since their introduction hundreds of years ago, nasturtiums have maintained a steady popularity. No self-respecting cottage garden could do without their vibrant colours – shades of orange, red and yellow – and easy ways. In more modern times they have continued to prove their worth. They need very little attention, which is a real bonus for those busy people with little gardening time.

When people think of nasturtiums they are usually picturing that annual favourite, *Tropaeolum majus* or the garden nasturtium. However, there are several others in the same genus, coming in three main groups; climbers, trailers and bedding varieties. Their versatility makes them ready, willing and able to adapt to life in any kind of container, a useful trait, especially if you are short of space.

It is possible to grow some as perennials, while others are too tender to survive all but the mildest of winters. Some have the lush, vibrant good looks of jungle creepers while even the more familiar garden nasturtium has several exotic varieties, such as 'Alaska',

Usually thought of as summer bedding plants, the ever obliging nasturtiums will fill all manner of unlikely nooks and crannies with warm, cheerful colour, whether the flowers are peeking out from beneath a hedge, clambering over a tree stump or cascading prettily in long trails down a wall or bank (above).

There are many more colours than orange and yellow in the nasturtium's palette. 'Peach Melba' (left) is a variety of Tropaeolum *majus* whose pale, creamy petals each have a blotch of orange at the base. In some varieties, extra colour is presented by the foliage; 'Alaska' (below) has leaves randomly splotched and veined with white and cream. Quite the most unusual colour in the genus, however, is provided by the heavenly blue notched petals of the rarely-grown climber Tropaeolum azureum (bottom).

with its splendid, marbled and blotched variegated foliage.

Several species are natural, born climbers. Perhaps the most unusual, in terms of colour, as well as one of the most difficult to find, is the herbaceous *Tropaeolum azureum*, which bears small, purple-blue flowers late in the summer. Although this plant is technically a perennial, it will not survive frost, so must be seen as an annual in areas where winter frosts are inevitable.

T. peregrinum, also known as *T. canariense*, is the well-known canary creeper –

RECOMMENDED VARIETIES

Climbers

T. majus 'Tall Mixed' are very vigorous and come in mixed colours. *T.* 'Spitfire' is equally vigorous but has orange flowers with red speckles, and the canary creeper (*Tropaeolum peregrinum*) has smaller, yellow flowers and may be grown as a perennial in mild climates.

Trailers

The 'Gleam' series of hybrids dominate this group. They have double or semi-double flowers and may be bought in mixed or single colours which include scarlet, yellow and orange.

Dwarfs

'Whirlybird' is the new favourite of this group. It comes in mixed or single colours and its flowers are held well above the foliage.

Other dwarf varieties include the 'Jewel' series, 'Empress of India', 'Alaska' and 'Peach Melba'.

named for its canary-yellow flowers rather than for any connection with the Canary Islands. This is another frost-tender plant that will only survive the winter in the mildest of climates. Its small, bright flowers are set off by grey-green leaves. It will grow to a height of 2m/6ft or more.

Hardy climbers

A frost-hardy climber is the flame creeper (*T. speciosum*). This member of the nasturtium family has striking red flowers in the summer months, followed by rather handsome, bright blue fruits nestling among the deep red remnants of the outer parts of the flowers, the calyces.

This lovely plant enjoys having its head in full sun but its roots in shade. It climbs to a height of 3m/10ft and is useful for covering fences, walls or dead trees. It is herbaceous,

Tropaeolum peregrinum, the canary creeper (above), is named for its delightful flowers, bright yellow with a feathery fringe. It is a tender perennial, but easily raised from seed and best treated as an annual. A vigorous climber, it will put on 2.4m/8ft of growth in a good season.

dying back to take a well-earned rest in winter.

T. tuberosum, 'Ken Aslet' is another handsome member of the nasturtium group of plants, with small red and orange trumpet-shaped flowers flourishing from mid-summer to autumn. It grows from tubers, as it name suggests, so although it is not frost-hardy, its tubers may be dug up and stored for next year. It is a particularly useful plant in exposed or coastal areas, as it will cheerfully put up with

The gorgeous colours of the single-flowered 'Whirlybird' series (top) have made this relatively new variety a great favourite among lovers of dwarf nasturtiums.

Many nasturtium varieties will happily climb or trail. This one's variegated leaves are set off to perfection if they are allowed to tumble lazily on to a paved patio (above).

wind and salt sprays.

Several other varieties will climb, including *T. majus* 'Tall Mixed' and *T. peltophorum* 'Spitfire'. These two varieties look lovely cascading down dry banks or swarming over unsightly constructions.

Trailers

This group is dominated by the *T. majus* 'Gleam' hybrids. The colours available include bright red, orange and yellow and may be bought as mixtures or in single colours.

These are the nasturtiums most suitable for use in hanging baskets or to trail over the front of window boxes and containers. Their bright colours and handsome leaves bring a cheerful, informal look to your garden or patio. They have double flowers and will grow to about 30-45cm/1-1½ft.

Bedding plants

All nasturtiums suitable for bedding plants are varieties of *T. majus*. 'Empress of India' grows to a height of 20cm/8in

and is vigorous and bushy in habit. Its dark crimson flowers give a fine show between early summer and autumn.

The 'Jewel' series of nasturtiums are particularly useful

Tropaeolum tuberosum (right) is a tender herbaceous climber whose tubers must be lifted and overwintered in a warm place if it is to survive the winter. However, it rewards the extra effort with handsome, trumpet-shaped, spurred, bi-coloured flowers that are produced in great profusion from the middle of summer through to the autumn.

The 'Gleam' series of T. majus *varieties have a trailing habit, making them the most popular choice for hanging baskets, window boxes or other raised containers. These double-flowered varieties, such as 'Golden Gleam' (right), are sold in the usual range of colours, either by the variety or in a mix.*

PERFECT PARTNERS

The perennial flame creeper (*T. speciosum*) dies back in winter. Planting it with a variegated ivy (above) sustains interest and cover.

as bedding plants because their semi-double flowers are held in plain view above the leaves. This is not always the case, and in many varieties the flowers can be hidden by exuberant foliage.

Another compact dwarf variety is 'Whirlybird': once again the flowers are held proudly above the foliage. The 'Whirlybird' series can be bought in mixed or single colours; all have simple, single flowers.

'Peach Melba' is another popular variety; it has pale yellow flowers blotched with scarlet. Like 'Jewel' and 'Whirlybird', this variety grows to about 30cm/1ft.

Simple needs

Most varieties of nasturtiums are really easy to please. The majority actually prefer poor soil, which means you are spared the trouble of preparing a special bed for them. All they require is a little elbow room and good drainage.

Propagation is simple, too. Annuals grow from seed, and basal cuttings can be taken from herbaceous varieties. Some grow from tubers and may be divided.

For *T. majus* varieties simply sow the seed in spring where the plants are to flower and keep the ground moist until the seedlings are established. If you want early colour, you can germinate your seeds in gentle heat during late winter and plant out when all threat of frost has passed.

Blackfly is the most likely pest; in fact, blackfly heaven is probably full of broad beans underplanted with nasturtiums. They can be controlled by spraying with an insecticide, but dousing them with soapy water is better – if a little less effective – if you want to encourage other, less destructive insects, like butterflies, into your garden.

Standard Roses

All gardens need to have a few aristocratic plants that are both distinctive and eye-catching. Standard roses are the upper crust of the rose world.

Standard roses are some of the most versatile plants in the garden and can be used in many ways. Placed amid a sea of shrub roses, they create a variation in height. They are equally superb as specimen plants in a lawn where they are highlighted against the plain green background. Weeping standards, with cascading branches, planted in a circular bed, create a particularly attractive feature.

If you have a front garden with flower beds on either side of a path, plant it with a number of standards spaced 1.2-1.5m/4-5ft apart, to create a beautiful avenue leading to the front door. Use them to create interesting height variations towards the back of a border. Standard roses can also be grown in containers.

What are standards?

Standard roses are the product of careful growing and grafting in nurseries. Both bush roses and standard roses have the same rootstock but standards are specially grown with a very long, bare stem topped by a head of foliage. Bush roses are grafted near the base while standards have three buds inserted about 90cm/3ft up the stem. In the following spring the old foliage is cut off and the new shoots develop to create the familiar lollipop shape of the modern standard. Budding takes place in late summer, using either the Ramanas rose (*Rosa rugosa*) or dog rose (*Rosa canina*) as rootstocks.

There are three types of standard roses and all have

their specific attractions. **Full standards** are usually just known as standards. Their branches develop about 1m/3½ft above the ground. **Half-standards** are slightly shorter, their branches starting at about 75cm/2½ft.

Generally, these are less widely availabale. **Weeping standards** are much taller and reach a height of 1.5-1.8m/5-6ft. The branches cascade and wire frames are used to train the shoots and spread them out evenly.

In town gardens, where space is often limited, a weeping standard is ideal. It needs only a small ground area but from its narrow stem there cascades a profusion of blooms.

The standard roses in this border (left) raise their elegant heads above the level of the surrounding flowers. Their thin stems must be well supported and they should be loosely secured to stakes in three places – at the base, in the middle and just below the point where the branches begin.

A traditional rose garden should include all types of rose and the standard takes pride of place, towering above the others in the border (right). Here reds and pinks do not clash but contrast beautifully in colour and texture.

As standards mature, like the 'Charlotte Elizabeth' (below), their stems become much thicker until they look almost like small trees. They require less attention as they age and need only an occasional trim to keep them in shape and prevent them becoming overgrown.

Standard roses like to be the centre of attention and so they need to be able to stand up to close scrutiny. If you take particular care when buying your rose, you will avoid disappointment later.

Buying your rose

If you are buying a bare-rooted plant, give the root system a thorough check before purchasing. There should be a minimum of three major roots, each at least 20cm/8in long.

The stem should be about 12mm/½in thick just below the point where the branches start. The head of the plant should be formed of at least two buds, not more than 10cm/4in apart and on opposite sides of the stem. Make sure that the plant is labelled.

Standard roses can be bought in two main forms. **Bare-rooted** plants are sold in winter during their dormant season. Normally they

are in wax-lined paper containers or wrapped in polythene to prevent the roots from drying out.

If you buy your rose when the soil in your garden is frozen or too wet for planting, leave the packing intact and stand the rose upright in a cool room or a shed. It can be left this way for up to 10 days.

Instant summer displays can be created by planting **container-grown** specimens which are already flowering when you purchase them. Container-grown roses should have been grown in the container for some time and should not have been recently transplanted from the open ground. Firm soil and a crusted, moss-covered surface are good signs to look out for.

Bare-rooted plants are less expensive than those grown in containers, but have a limited planting time. Container-grown roses, though they cost

True to its name, 'Fragrant Cloud' (above) is particularly heavily scented.

The breathtaking 'Iceberg' rose (left) has small, perfectly formed white blooms.

For something really unusual choose the paper-textured Rosa gallica 'Versicolor' (below). The Rosa gallica species also includes some striking spotted varieties.

more, can be planted at any time of year.

For a really spectacular display, plant roses in abundance, harmonizing standard roses with the colours of the surrounding rose bushes. Strong colours, such as carmine, deep pink or bright red associate beautifully with the palest of roses in whites and creams with just the faintest hint of apricot or lemon.

Colour blending

For a more dazzling effect take advantage of the bright colours which are available and choose a vibrant scheme of sunny yellow with crimsons or scarlets, vivid oranges with apricots, and brownish-reds or scarlet-crimson with pale yellow or pink. For something more subtle mix pale yellows and creams with soft pinks or blends of gold. Lavender, lilac and mauve associate wonderfully with yellow, white and

cream. Salmon pink and oranges are enhanced by pale golds, yellows and pale pinks.

Roses can look as splendid with other plants as they do with other roses. Some combinations are particularly effective for extra colour and visual impact.

White roses create a cool, fresh atmosphere when planted within an edging of the dwarf, green-leaved box (*Buxus sempervirens* 'Suffruticosa'). It is an ideal duo for a formal-looking garden. The hardy arum lily (*Zantedeschia aethiopica* 'Crowborough') completes the picture.

Perfect partners

Pink and blush-shaded roses are superbly partnered by the low-growing, evergreen rosemary (*Rosmarinus officinalis* 'Severn Sea'), which has the added bonus of beautifully aromatic leaves and brilliant blue flowers in spring, then sporadically until late in the year. Lavender is another good partner plant for these roses. Its leaves are grey-green and the violet-coloured flowers open in early summer.

Highlight an apricot-yellow standard rose by underplanting it with the grey-green leaved nepeta (*N.* × *faassenii*), which has spires of lavender-blue flowers all summer or the herbaceous, silvery lamb's ear (*Stachys olympica*, also known as *S. lanata*).

If you choose one of the unusual blue-pink roses, sur-

round it with an edging mixture of the bluish-grey leaved rue (*Ruta graveolens*), sky-blue garden panies (*Viola* × *wittrockiana*) and lavender.

Planting a standard

The procedure for planting bare-rooted and container-grown standard roses is slightly different, but for either type prepare your planting site as far in advance as possible, to enable the soil to settle. Dig the soil deeply, removing the roots of perennial weeds and breaking up the sub-soil to ensure good drainage.

If your soil is extremely acidic you may need to add lime to make it more balanced as roses prefer only slight acidity. Take care not to apply excessive amounts of lime. Follow the directions on the packet very carefully.

Bare-rooted specimens

First cut off any leaves and fruit and remove any weak shoots. Cut off damaged or excessively long roots and stand the rose in a bucket of water for at least two hours. Dig a

As its pompon-like blossoms spill over carelessly, the weeping standard 'Dorothy Perkins' (above) gives an air of carefree abandon to the garden. Weeping standards are the tallest and least formal standards and they fit into a country garden particularly well.

This standard (right) captures the country charm and formality of the garden. The border is full of simple plants like lavender and campion and the blooms of the rose continue this theme but the whole effect, complete with box hedge and intricate topiary specimen, is elegant and stylish.

hole wide enough to accommodate the roots, and to a depth that enables the old soil-mark on the stem to be positioned slightly deeper than the surrounding soil. This allows for subsequent soil settlement. Insert a stake (3cm/1¼in thick and 45cm/18in taller than the first branches) into the centre of the hole. The stake should have been treated with a plant friendly wood preservative.

Spread out the roots and cover with loose topsoil, firming it in layers until it is level with the surrounding soil. Add fertilizer in the spring. Secure the stem to the stake in three places and leave the ties slightly loose. Ensure that the plant is labelled.

Container-grown roses
When planting a container-grown standard it is essential that the roots are not unduly disturbed. Follow the basic procedure for planting a bare-rooted rose but take note of these points:
- Water the plant thoroughly three hours before planting.
- Ensure the plant is well supported by a strong stake.
- Firm a mixture of topsoil and peat plus a sprinkling of bone meal around the soil ball.
- Water the soil regularly until the plant is established, especially during dry weather.

Taking care
In autumn, lightly fork a little sulphate of potash around the plant, following the manufacturer's recommendations.

In spring, lightly hoe in a general rose fertilizer, and do this again in midsummer. Do not apply fertilizers later than this, as it encourages lush, frost-sensitive growth.

Dead-head roses as soon as the blooms fade and mulch your standard rose in spring. Water the soil thoroughly, then place a 5cm/2in thick layer of well-rotted manure or garden compost around the plant. Always apply spring fertilizers before you mulch.

Keep a lookout for rogue buds and remove them by rubbing them with your fingers. You must also remove suckers growing from the roots and main stem of the plant.

PRUNING STANDARDS
The way you should prune your standard rose will depend on its age and type.
- Established standard roses should be pruned in spring. The buds will have swelled but leaves will not have developed. Use sharp secateurs and cut to outward-budding points.
- Newly-planted standards should have their shoots cut back to about 20cm/8in. Older plants need less severe pruning.
- Weeping standards need hard pruning in spring to encourage the development of long, cascading shoots. Cut back the branches to about 15cm/6in long at the top of the stem.
- Trim back long shoots of all standard roses in early winter.

This half-standard, 'The Fairy' (left), is ideal for container growing. Placed near other plants there is an interesting contrast in scale and it provides flowers at a height without taking up space lower down. The plants around the base hide the stem of the standard rose.

The grey-green leaves of lavender compliment the salmon-pink petals of the 'Memento' rose (below). Their delicate fragrances combine as harmoniously as their colours.

DRASTIC MEASURES
Neglected standards can quickly become unsightly. Suckers at ground-level and on stems will soon dominate plants. If varieties budded on Ramanas rose (*Rosa rugosa*) stocks are neglected over many years, they will not be worth keeping but those budded on dog rose rootstocks tend to be more resilient. The whole plant may be overwhelmed by the root part and reveal a mass of single, magenta-pink flowers amid light green leaves on very prickly stems. Dig up and remove. As a re-cycling measure, however, they could be replanted to form an attractive, flowering boundary hedge.

Clematis

The clematis genus contains many of the very best climbing plants, producing attractive flowers in an enormous variety of shapes and colours.

If ever a plant deserved the title 'Queen of Climbers', clematis does. This handsome genus of plants offers literally hundreds of gorgeous varieties. The choice of flower colour ranges from subtle, pastel shades of pink, blue and mauve, to the more regal hues of crimson, magenta and purple. Rich creams are available, as are stunning whites and vibrant yellows.

Some varieties produce an abundance of small, delicate, single or double blooms, while others have fewer, but more imposing flowers. Some have seed heads so beautiful that they are much sought after for flower arrangements.

Clever clematis

The clematis family can supply a glorious climber suitable for virtually any site. Exposed, chilly, north-facing walls are absolutely no problem to *C. alpina* or *C. macropetala* varieties, for example, while an ugly shed, wall or outbuilding can soon be camouflaged by any member of the vigorous *C. montana* branch of the family.

Clematis will clothe and soften the outlines of arches and pergolas with enchanting displays of flowers. By selecting your varieties carefully, you can have blooms from spring to autumn.

Trees and shrubs whose interest is limited to early spring need not be an embarrassment for the rest of the season. You can grow a clematis through them. Varieties of *C. jackman-*

The early summer blooms of 'Nelly Moser' are best in semi-shade; the carmine stripe fades in full sun.

PLANT PROFILE

Suitable site and soil Likes a deep, moist, cool root run. Will thrive in almost any good quality garden soil. Sandy or chalky soils must have plenty of organic matter added to help retain moisture. Do not plant too near to thirsty hedges (especially privet) or trees as these will rob the clematis of moisture. Clematis appreciates a bit of lime, but it is not essential.

Planting Container grown clematis may be planted at any time as long as the soil retains some warmth. Early autumn or late spring are best.

Cultivation and care When, where and how to prune depends on the variety; read the instructions carefully when you buy.

Clematis must be fed regularly with a liquid fertilizer in the growing season. In autumn, mulch with farmyard manure or work in bone meal around the stem.

Propagation Cuttings are best left to the professional. Layering in summer is an easier method. Fill a 10-15cm/4-6in flowerpot with cutting compost and sink into the ground a little away from the parent so you do not damage roots. Bend a young shoot until it touches the soil in the pot. Make a slit upwards from below a leaf node, and dust it with hormone rooting powder. Cover with soil and clip into place with a bent piece of wire. Cover with a stone or slate to keep pot moist and cool. Keep pot damp. Sever the young plant from the parent the following spring and plant in the usual way.

Pests and diseases Clematis wilt tends to attack young plants. Remove and destroy infected stems immediately. With luck new stems will form. Spraying the leaves and soaking the immediate root area with a benomyl fungicide will help to protect new growth. If you lose your plant, replace the surface soil at the site and grow a different variety. If the trouble persists, plant a species clematis in new soil, as they are less susceptible than cultivated varieties.

Mildew may be a problem, especially to some hybrids. Spray with a proprietary fungicide.

ii and *C. viticelli* are useful for this. *C. montana* is a particularly handy choice if you wish to cover a large tree or to disguise a dead one.

Clematis can be used as ground cover. Once again *C. montana* may be called into service. Other suitable subjects are varieties of *C. alpina*, *C. macropetala*, *C. orientalis* and *C. tangutica*. Any of these plants also look lovely if allowed to tumble down a bank.

There are even a few herbaceous species suitable for the mixed border, including *C. integrifolia* and *C. recta*.

Flowering types

There are so many species and varieties of clematis that it is useful to split them into three groups, depending on the season when they flower, their growing habit and their pruning requirements.

The first group includes the *Clematis montana* varieties, along with *C. macropetala* and

There is great variety in the shapes, as well as the colours, of clematis flowers. The late flowering, pendulous, golden yellow blooms of C. tangutica (above) have a lantern shape, while the summer flowers of the herbaceous, late-flowering C. integrifolia (left) are deep blue bells. These are succeeded later in the year by very attractive, light-brown seed heads. The most readily recognizable of all clematis flower forms, though, are the abundant, flat, single blooms of C. montana (right) which appear in late spring.

C. alpina. All are vigorous, fully hardy, and produce masses of blooms in late spring. Pruning should be restricted to merely tidying up the plant. Dead flower heads and stems should be removed immediately after flowering so the new growth ripens before winter.

C. montana 'Elizabeth' can reach a height of 10-12m/30-40ft and bears soft pink, scented flowers, while *C. m.* 'Tetrarose' is a stronger, satin pink variety that reaches a height of 7-8m/23-26ft.

Macropetala and alpina varieties are good looking and very hardy. *C. macropetala* 'Markham's Pink' has delicate, bell-shaped flowers in a glorious dusky pink. It grows to a height of 3m/10ft and blooms appear in late spring and summer. It is a suitable clematis for a small garden.

C. alpina 'Frances Rivis' is a lovely bell-shaped variety in a mid-blue colour. 'Ruby' has purplish-pink blooms. They are free flowering in spring with an occasional second flush in summer. The delicate, fluffy, silver seed heads are produced in the summer months. These varieties also suit small gardens, reaching a height of 2-3m/6-10ft.

Early flowers

The second group includes early flowering, frost hardy subjects. These should be pruned back to the lowest pair of strong buds in their first season, so that growth is more vigorous. In subsequent seasons, pruning should be restricted to removing dead growth only, because the flowers are only produced on the previous year's stems.

'Nelly Moser' is an old favourite in this group. It produces large, single, flat rose coloured flowers that have a carmine stripe on each petal. Blooms appear in early summer on plants that reach a height of 3.5m/11ft. The flower colours fade in strong sunlight so it is best to plant these in a shaded east, west or north facing site.

'Proteus' has wide, double mauve-pink flowers. This handsome variety produces blooms in early summer and a second flush of single flowers later in the season. It reaches

RECOMMENDED VARIETIES

'Crimson King'. Height 2.4-3m/8-10ft. Has large, striking, clear crimson flowers in summer and autumn.

C. alpina 'Willy'. Height 2-3m/6-10ft. Has delicate white, lantern-shaped flowers in abundance in spring. Flowers have an attractive pinkish flush at the base. Suits north facing and exposed sites.

'Elsa Späth'. Height 2-3m/6-10ft. Has masses of deep mauve-blue, single flowers throughout summer.

C. montana 'Elizabeth' reaches a height of 10-12m/30-40ft and bears soft pink, scented flowers.

C. macropetala 'Markham's Pink' has delicate, bell-shaped dusky pink flowers and grows to a height of 3m/10ft.

'Nelly Moser' has large, single, flat, rose coloured flowers with a carmine stripe on each petal. It reaches a height of 3.5m/11ft.

C. orientalis has deep yellow, bell-shaped flowers between late summer and autumn. Grows to 3-6m/10-20ft and requires hard pruning early in the year.

'Vyvyan Pennell' is one of the best doubles. Has lavender or violet flowers with magnificent, golden yellow anthers. Height 2.4-3m/8-10ft.

The alpine clematis (C. alpina) *is the best choice for very exposed sites. The blooms of 'Frances Rivis' (above left) are enhanced by a cluster of white stamens – looking very much like petals – in the centre.*

'Vyvyan Pennell' produces large, double flowers (above) in early summer, followed by a later flush of single, slightly darker blooms.

The semi-double blooms of C. macropetala are small, just 5cm/2in across, but make up in numbers what they lack in size (above right).

The yellow flowers of C. orientalis (right) appear in late summer.

a height of 2.4-3m/8-10ft.

'Rouge Cardinale' flowers on new wood only, so it needs hard pruning every year. This lovely variety produces masses of velvety, crimson, single flowers in summer and makes an excellent subject for small gardens, growing to a height of 2.4-3m/8-10ft.

'Henryi' is a vigorous plant that boasts lovely, white, single flowers with handsome, chocolate coloured anthers that contrast well with the petals. Flowers appear in summer on a plant that reaches a height of 3m/10ft.

Spring pruning

The third group produces large, flattish flowers in late summer and early autumn. All

'Proteus' is another variety which has a first flush of double flowers with a greenish tint to the outer petals (left), followed by a second of single blooms.

One of the more unusual forms of clematis is C. florida 'Sieboldii' (right), whose flat, star-shaped blooms resemble those of the passion flower. The petals, usually described as creamy-white, can have a green flush, as here, and the central mound is made up of stamens which mature from green to purple.

The crimson petals of 'Rouge Cardinal' (below) have a lovely, soft, velvety texture.

are frost hardy. This group is dominated by 'Jackmanii' varieties. It is very important to prune these annually because the flowers are borne on new growth. For best results, cut them back to the lowest two or three strong buds on each stem in early spring.

C. viticella 'Purpurea Plena Elegans' is a gorgeous variety with double, rose-purple flowers that form tight rosettes. Sometimes the outer petals are green. It reaches a height of 3-4m/10-12ft.

'Jackmanii Superba' grows to about the same height. A vigorous plant, it has large, single, deep purple blooms.

C. florida 'Sieboldii' is really only suitable for a very shel-

tered site as it is a bit weak and tender. What it lacks in vigour it makes up for in beauty, however. The flowers are creamy white, with rich, purple stamens. It reaches a height of 2-3m/6-10ft.

Caring for clematis
Clematis like a deep, rich, moist and cool root run. Although they will thrive in almost any good quality, well-cultivated garden soil, good preparation is essential if you want your plant to flower profusely and live long.

Dig a hole 45cm/18in square and deep. Fork over the subsoil at the base and add two or three handfuls of bone meal. Next, add a fairly generous layer of well-rooted manure. Then fill the hole with a mixture of rich garden compost or John Innes No 3, some peat or peat substitute and sand.

Place the crown 5-8cm/2-3in below soil level, burying the first pair of leaves or nodes. Top off with tiles, stones or a thick mulch to keep roots cool and to retain moisture.

Feeding time
Clematis are hungry plants and it pays to feed them regularly as they will soon exhaust the nutrients provided at

HOT HEADS

Many clematis like their feet in the shade and their heads in the sun. All of them like cool roots; place tiles, stones or slates around the stems to keep the ground cool.

Although it is not essential for their well-being, clematis like lime. Covering the roots with a piece of limestone allows some of the mineral to leech into the ground.

planting. Mulch with farmyard manure in autumn or work in some bone meal around the stem. Provide sulphate of potash in spring and feed with a liquid fertilizer every two weeks during the growing season.

Make sure that your plant never goes thirsty by watering during dry spells and by providing a good, thick layer of mulch to prevent the evaporation of precious water from the soil when the sun shines.

Support your clematis

Clematis require support. They do not attach themselves to walls the way ivy does, but twine, so they need something to twine around, either another, preferably woody, plant or an artificial support.

When you wish to clothe a wall or fence, use a trellis or a framework of 23cm/9in squares made with plastic covered wire. Make sure that there is a gap of 1cm/½in between the support and the wall. When planting, allow a gap of at least 30cm/1ft between the clematis and the wall.

If you want a clematis to scramble through a tree, plant it outside the overhang of the branches on the north side.

Bridge the gap between your clematis and the wall or tree with a cane, placed at an angle, so that the plant may twine its way along it to its permanent support.

PERFECT PARTNERS

The twining habit of clematis makes them adept at climbing through other plants.

Here, *C.* × *jackmanii* 'Superba' is supported by a double shrub rose.

Chrysanthemums

From tiny alpines to cottagey daisies and the handsome blooms of the show tents, chrysanthemums give us an outstanding range of flower forms and colours.

As summer beds begin to fade, the chrysanthemums come into their own. From late summer right through to the onset of winter, these magnificient plants provide a spectrum of brilliant colour that echoes the flaming hues of autumn.

Their enormous popularity is well earned. The diversity of flower shape and size from the huge, flawless globes nurtured for exhibition to the small, smiling daisy-like faces at the edge of a border, is exceptional, while their long flowering season and lasting blooms ensure a continuing array of almost every imaginable colour and hue. Chrysanthemums will grace borders, tubs and window boxes, as well as making good indoor pot plants.

Eastern origins

Chrysanthemums have been cultivated and admired in the Orient since 500 B.C., but it was not until late in the 18th century that they first came to Europe, brought from China by a French navigator.

In 1843, the Royal Horticultural Society sent the famous plant collector, Robert Fortune, to the Far East in search of new species, and some of his discoveries became the forebears of many of today's modern chrysanthemums.

The cultivation of modern varieties for exhibition is an exciting and all-consuming passion for a large number of enthusiasts, professional and amateur alike. These plants, though, are only part of a very large and diverse group.

The genus has been broken

up in recent years, with species allocated to new genera, but, since these are not yet in common usage, we shall continue to love them as chrysanthemums. All have their individual virtues and delights, and all deserve consideration for a place in our gardens.

The modern garden varieties give us the greatest range of flower shapes and vibrant, jewel-like colours. They are classified according to the time at which they flower: early-flowering varieties bloom from late summer; late-flowering from the middle of autumn.

Late-flowering varieties are grown in pots, standing outside during the summer then being brought in to flower in the greenhouse. In temperate climates, only the early flowers will bloom successfully in the garden.

Flower forms

Modern chrysanthemums are also classified by the form and size of the flower and whether they are borne singly or in sprays (see box page 1090).

Large blooms are achieved

The public face of the chrysanthemum is represented by the extravagant blooms of the modern varieties (left), seen on the show bench or in florists.

'Pennine Gambol' (above) is anemone-centred, with several layers of ray florets surrounding a large, raised centre.

Korean chrysanthemums, like many others, are now classified as members of the genus Dendranthema. However, despite their obvious charms, few varieties are offered for sale under any name. 'Raquel' (right) is a rare exception.

through disbudding: all but four or five flower buds are nipped out, so all the plant's energy is channelled into producing sizeable blooms on stems reaching 1-1.5m/3-5ft in height. Though mostly grown for cutting or exhibiting, the reflexed form is excellent in the garden, shedding the rain from its downward-curving petals or florets. 'Brietner' is a lovely pink variety; 'Bruera' a superb white.

Spray and pompon chrysanthemums bring an invaluable abundance of smaller flowers to borders, and provide some of the best cut flowers for the home. They are generally shorter and bushier plants (though sprays can grow to

RECOMMENDED VARIETIES

Nurseries have to make their selections from a vast number of varieties cultivated today. Consequently, you will have to make your own choices from those available to you locally or by post. Here are some you may find without too much difficulty.

Early-flowering Reflexed: 'Brietner' (pink); 'Bruera' (white); 'Alice Jones' (light bronze); 'Yvonne Arnaud' (cerise).

Intermediate: 'Bill Wade' (white); 'Ginger Nut' (light red-bronze). Sprays: 'Margaret' (pink double); 'Lemon Margaret' (pale yellow double); 'Pennine Gambol' (pink anemone); 'Pennine Tango' (bronze single). Pompons: 'Bronze Fairie' (bronze); 'Cameo' (white); 'Jante Wells' (yellow). Also, do try the very rewarding Korean hybrids.

Hardy perennials
Chrysanthemum rubellum: 'Clara Curtis' (clear pink); 'Mary Stoker' (soft yellow); 'Duchess of Edinburgh' (bright crimson). Shasta daisy (*C. maximum*): 'Wirral Supreme' and 'Esther Read' (double white); 'Phyllis Smith' (fringed white petals with almost shredded effect); 'Snowcap' (small variety, to about 45cm/1½ft).

Annuals Marguerite (*C. frutescens*, syn. *Argyranthemum frutescens*): 'Jamaica Primrose' (soft yellow); 'Mary Wootton' (pink). Feverfew (*C. parthenium*, syn. *Matricaria eximia*): 'Aureum' (white flowers and gold-tinted foliage). *C. carinatum* (syn. *C. tricolor*): 'Court Jesters' (concentric rings of contrasting colours in numerous combinations).

1.2m/4ft) and are not disbudded since their beauty lies in the sheer number of flowers.

The sprays have various flower forms, while pompoms bear small, globe- or button-shaped blooms. Together they offer a kaleidoscopic range of colours, from the single bronze flowers of the spray variety, 'Pennine Tango', to the pink, anemone-centred sprays of 'Pennine Gambol' and the yellow pompons of 'Jante Wells'.

Korean chrysanthemums are, sadly, not easily found nowadays but are well worth looking for, since they continue to provide colour when the early-flowering varieties are starting to look a little battered. They are bushy plants, growing to about 60cm/2ft and clothed in sprays of small flowers in gorgeous hues.

All these varieties need to be lifted and stored away from damaging frosts. There are species, however, which are fully hardy and happy to remain in the garden throughout the year.

Daisy flowers

Chrysanthemum rubellum is compact and bushy, about 45-75cm/1½-2½ft in height, and covered from late summer

The clear pink single blooms of C. rubellum (or Dendranthema) 'Clara Curtis' (left) are so abundant, the dense, bushy foliage almost disappears.

The feverfew (C. parthenium) is a perennial usually treated as an annual. Here (below) it is growing through a clump of irises.

At the other end of the floral spectrum from the showy modern varieties is the tiny alpine C. hosmariense (right above).

The pyrethrums may be found as C. coccineum, Pyrethrum roseum or Tanacetum coccineum. The species is not encountered, but the colourful hybrids (right) are a staple of summer flower beds.

The marguerite (C. frutescens syn. Argyranthemum frutescens) is a tender perennial, in demand for containers as well as beds and borders. 'Jamaica Primrose' (right below) is an excellent variety.

through autumn with clusters of single flowers in a cheerful array of colours. One of the oldest varieties, and still deservedly popular, is the delightful 'Clara Curtis' which has lovely, clear pink, golden-centred blooms.

The Shasta daisy (*Chrysanthemum maximum*), a relative of our wild ox-eye daisies, has long been a popular garden resident, cherished for its large white flowers borne singly through summer. Sometimes classified as *C. × superbum*, 'Wirral Supreme' and 'Esther Read' are much-loved varieties with double flowers. About 1m/3ft tall, Shasta daisies look splendid with golden-flowered neighbours.

Chrysanthemum coccineum is more commonly known as pyrethrum (*Pyrethrum roseum*). It is lovely in borders, with single or double flowers on long stems (60-90cm/2-3ft tall), and an array of colours from white through pink to red, accentuated by attractively feathery foliage.

There are even alpine species for rock gardens, such as *Chrysanthemum hosmariense*, just 20cm/8in tall, with white flowers set against finely-cut

silvery green leaves, or the even smaller, pink-flowered *C. weyrichii* (4-6in/10-15cm).

Annuals

Annuals, of course, are invaluable for adding shots of colour quickly and easily. *C. carinatum* (syn. *C. tricolor*) provides stunning, rainbow hues and attractive, feathery foliage. The flat, daisy-like, summer flowers, borne singly on erect stems 60cm/2ft tall have dark purplish centres surrounded by ray petals decorated with concentric rings of contrasting colours. 'Court Jesters' gives large flowers with a magnificent colour range.

Though a perennial, feverfew (*C. parthenium* syn. *Matricaria eximia*) is short-lived, and commonly grown as an annual. 'Aureum' is a lovely variety with fragrant, golden tinted foliage and small, daisy-like white flowers in summer and early autumn. A bushy plant, 20-45cm/8-18in high, it makes a neat edging for bor-

'Phyllis Smith' (above) is a variety of C. maximum with particularly ragged ray florets and a handsome, golden, central dome.

'Bronze Fairie' (left) is an early-flowering modern variety which boasts perfectly formed pompon blooms that are just 4cm/1¹/₂in across.

'Yvonne Arnaud' (right) is another modern early flowering variety. This time the flowers are reflexed, and much larger than those of 'Bronze Fairie', reaching 12cm/5in in diameter.

Jolly 'Court Jesters', with their multi-coloured flowers, do not fit into formal schemes and are best used in a riotous mixed bed with other annuals like nicotiana and mignonette.

ders and a splendidly decorative addition to containers.

The marguerite (*C. frutescens*, syn. *Argyranthemum frutescens*) has recently seen a revival in popularity, and is another excellent choice for tubs and containers, bearing a profusion of white, yellow or pink daisies through summer and into autumn.

Chrysanthemum care

While those who grow chrysanthemums for exhibition have their own recipes for success, there is really no mystery surrounding these versatile plants in the garden. They like sun and fertile, well-drained soil, and dislike very acid and waterlogged sites. Some shelter from winds is helpful for the taller varieties which also benefit from support with canes or peasticks. Chrysanthemums are prone to a number of pests and diseases, but regular spraying should take care of these.

After flowering, cut all the hardy perennial chrysanthemums back to ground level.

Early-flowering modern varieties need a little more attention. Plant them out once the danger of severe frosts has passed, then, just under two weeks later, pinch out the growing tip to channel the plant's energy into its side shoots. These will produce healthy 'breaks' which will eventually bear the blooms.

The size of the flower will depend to a large extent on the number of breaks that are allowed to develop. In the garden, about four to six breaks produce the best results, so you should remove any others as they appear. For disbuds, also remove any side-shoots which emerge on the lengthening breaks.

In midsummer, the flower buds appear on the top of each break, surrounded by a cluster of smaller buds. Take off these smaller buds, leaving just the central one, if you want large blooms. After flowering, cut them back to about 20cm/8in, then lift for storage over winter away from frosts.

SAFETY FIRST

COVER UP

Chrysanthemum leaves can cause allergic reactions such as soreness or itching of the skin. If you think you may be affected, avoid skin contact by wearing gloves and keeping your arms and legs covered when working with them.

Tulips

Among the most satisfying of all bulbs, tulips provide a gorgeous array of flower shapes and colours that are full of the joys of spring.

Tulips have been gracing gardens for a very long time. They were first introduced into Europe from the Ottoman Empire in the late 16th century and have flourished there ever since.

In the early days, there was a great craze for the plants that forced up the prices of many varieties until only the very wealthy could afford them. At the height of this mania, single bulbs occasionally sold for more than an ordinary man could expect to earn in a lifetime.

However, as time went on, commercial growers managed to produce bulbs at prices that would suit all but the emptiest of pockets.

Over the centuries, tulips have been produced in a vast array of colours, from pastel pinks, yellows and creamy whites to rich, oriental shades of deep purples, vibrant yellows and fiery reds and oranges. Some are single coloured, while others are bi-coloured and boast handsome feathering or bold stripes. There are also less common varieties that have intriguing mottles and blotches.

Flower shape varies quite a bit too. The elegantly simple, upright, six-petalled conical cups that most people associate with tulips is just one variation. Others, such as *Tulipa turkestanica* and *T. biflora*, are fringed or frilled. Lily-flowered varieties have long, pointed petals that often turn outwards at the tips, while there are several elaborate double forms.

There are so many to choose from that horticulturists have

found it necessary to divide tulips into as many as 15 separate groups or divisions (see box on page 1210).

An early start
It is possible to have tulips flowering in your garden from early spring right through into early summer.

The first spring bulbs appear at the very moment when most people are heartily sick of winter. The sight of the first tulips signal that spring has arrived and that scarves and gloves can be joyously abandoned. For spirit-lifting purposes alone, early tulips are a must in any garden. Many of

The single, bowl-shaped, bi-coloured flowers of the Darwin hybrid, 'Beauty of Appledoorn' (above), appearing in mid to late spring, typify the simple beauty of the Tulipa genus.

Suitable site and soil Tulips like a sunny site. Short varieties look good in rockeries. Both short and tall varieties do well in containers. They prefer alkaline soil but will tolerate virtually any type.

Planting Plant bulbs nose up in holes at least 15cm/ 6in deep and 10cm/4in apart. Add bone meal as a top dressing or sprinkle a little in each hole.

Cultivation and care When flowering is over, dead head and provide a liquid feed until the foliage has died back. Either lift the bulbs for storage in a cool dry place or leave in, if they are planted deeply.

Propagation Remove the offsets and store in a cool, dry place until autumn. Plant in nursery beds until they mature. Plump bulblets may flower the next year, others may take up to three years to develop. Feed in the usual way. May be propagated by seed, but this can take up to seven years. There is no guarantee that hybrid varieties will come true.

Pests and diseases Stem and bulb eelworm causes twisted and deformed growth. Infested bulbs are soft, with a white woolly growth at the base. Destroy infected plants and bulbs and do not replant the site for three years.

Tulip fire is the most common and most serious disease. Spray with an appropriate fungicide such as benomyl at the first sign of grey, scorched patches on the foliage. If only a few plants are infected it is as well to lift and destroy them. Do not replant the same spot with tulips. Aphids may also cause trouble; spray with soapy water or a proprietary insecticide.

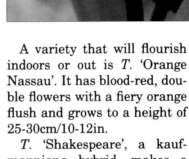

these varieties are suitable for forcing indoors, where they will flower very early indeed.

Several of the 15 divisions offer early-flowering varieties. Some are long-stemmed and make wonderfully elegant cut flowers for the home. *Tulipa* 'Diana', for instance, has large, white, single flowers carried on strong stems which reach a height of 28cm/11in, excellent for cutting.

Tulips have other, less well-known, flower shapes. The blooms of T. turkestanica (above) have a more open, star shape, while lily-flowered varieties, such as 'Queen of Sheba' (below left) have long, outward-curving petals. Double varieties, such as 'Angélique' (below right) may more closely resemble peonies.

A variety that will flourish indoors or out is *T.* 'Orange Nassau'. It has blood-red, double flowers with a fiery orange flush and grows to a height of 25-30cm/10-12in.

T. 'Shakespeare', a kauf-manniana hybrid, makes a good subject for containers or the front of spring borders, as it grows to a mere 12-15cm/5-6in high. Its blooms are a deep red, edged with salmon on the outside. The inside is salmon, flushed with red with a splash of yellow at the base.

If you would like a more unusual tulip to grace your early spring garden, choose either *T. humilis* or *T. violacea* to plant in your rock garden or raised bed. These two are hard to tell apart, as they both have open flowers in a lovely shade of magenta, with a rich yellow at the centre. The petals are

elegantly tapered and both these lovely plants will reach a height of 20cm/8in.

Betwixt and between

A number of tulips will bloom after the earliest but before the late comers. These are very useful because they tend to burst forth at the point when many other spring bulbs have passed their best.

'Orange Emperor' (right) is a fosteriana hybrid, flowering in early to mid spring. The orange and yellow blooms grow 16in/40cm tall.

The various parrot hybrids are deeply frilled, twisted and often rather loud. 'Flaming Parrot' (below) is one of the most clamorously coloured of them all.

T. whittallii is unusual for a tulip in that each stem may have up to four blooms, rather than the usual one. The petals are a bright brownish-orange and handsomely tapered to produce an oval shape. It grows to 30-35cm/12-14in tall.

The horned tulip (*T. acuminata*) is very elegant, with petals tapering to long, thin points. This lovely, tall (30-45cm/12-18in) variety is either pale red or yellow, with a slight flush of red or green on the outside of the petals.

Another lofty variety is *T.* 'Gordon Cooper', a Darwin hybrid which reaches 60cm/2ft, making it excellent for flower arrangements and for the middle or back of a border. It has rich, pink blooms with a hint of red at the edges. Inside, the petals are red with yellow and blue bases.

Here comes summer

Late tulips herald the coming of summer; some even continue flowering into the early part of the season.

This can cause a problem. As with all bulbs, it is important to allow tulips' foliage to die back naturally after flowering so that the bulb can gather strength for the next year's growth. Late flowering tulips can make beds and borders look untidy when they reach this stage, taking up valuable summer bedding space. You can overcome this by planting in containers or by lifting them after flowering and replanting them in an out-of-the-way trench to die back.

T. 'Angélique' is a double-flowered tulip that, though classified as late, makes a fine spring bedding plant. Its pink flowers open wide to resemble a peony. It is delicately scented and grows to a height of 40cm/16in. It is best to plant this one in a sheltered position

PERFECT PARTNERS

The rich colours of 'Black Parrot' are set off well by silver-grey leaves, here provided by the cardoon *(Cynara cardunculus)*.

T. pulchella, *otherwise known as* T. humilis pulchella *(above), produces its purplish flowers with black or yellow centres in early spring. As it grows to just 8in/20cm tall, it makes an excellent subject for a rockery or a small container.*

as it tends to be top heavy and may be damaged by winds.

For a really fancy, bi-coloured plant, *T.* 'Estella Rijnveld', a member of the parrot class, is hard to beat. The flowers are red, streaked with white and touches of green, and it has distinctive frilled or fringed petals that twist to give a somewhat crumpled appearance. It is a tall plant, some 60cm/2ft high.

The darkest of all tulips, *T.* 'Queen of the Night', can bring drama to your garden. The deep maroon, almost black, single flowers appear in late spring or early summer. The blooms are long-lasting and are carried 60cm/2ft tall on long, sturdy stems.

Tulip bulbs are easy to obtain at most garden centres

THE GREAT DIVIDE

Horticulturists group tulips in 15 divisions according to size, flowering time and flower type. The heights given are maximums.

(1) Single early. Flower in early-mid spring. Height 38cm/15in.

(2) Double early. Long-lasting, double flowers early to mid spring. Height 38cm/15in.

(3) Triumph. Sturdy stems and single flowers in mid to late spring. Height 50cm/20in.

(4) Darwin hybrids. Large, single flowers, mid to late spring. Height 75cm/30in.

(5) Single late. Single flowers of variable shape in late spring to early summer. Height 63cm/25in.

(6) Lily flowered. Elegant single flowers with very pointed petals in late spring. Height 75cm/30in.

(7) Fringed. Petal tops are fringed. Height 75cm/30in.

(8) Viridflora. Shape varies but petals have green markings in late spring. Height 45cm/18in.

(9) Rembrandt. Single, striped or feathered flowers in late spring. Some ancient varieties. Height 60cm/2ft.

(10) Parrot. Large single flowers with frilled or fringed edges in late spring. Height 60cm/2ft.

(11) Double late, peony flowered. Bowl shaped, double flowers in late spring. Height 60cm/2ft.

(12) Kaufmanniana hybrids. Single, often bi-coloured blooms in early spring. Height 25cm/10in.

(13) Fosteriana hybrids. Large single flowers in early spring. Leaves often striped or mottled. Height 60cm/2ft.

(14) Greigii hybrids. Large, single flowers in early spring, leaves always mottled or striped. Height 30cm/12in.

(15) Others. Species and hybrids that do not fit the other categories.

bulbs. It is best to avoid any that are already shooting. Make certain that the skins show no signs of disease or damage. Tulip bulbs bruise easily, so handle them with care. Avoid any that are soft and spongy to the touch, as they may have a fungal disease.

Planting

The best time to plant tulips is in late autumn, a while after planting your other bulbs. This late start helps to make sure that new shoots will not be damaged by frost.

It is best not to plant tulips in the same site year after year, so ring the changes if you can. If you have limited space you could plant your tulips in containers; many smaller varieties are suitable for window-boxes. Another option is to replace the top soil of your bed every four or five years. A mix of good humus, peat or peat

'Prinses Irene' (above) is an early flowering single tulip with an attractive and unusual colouring; the orange flowers are irregularly streaked with purple. It grows 30-35cm/12-14in tall.

The large, flamboyant, frilly flowers of 'Estella Rijnveld' (left) mark it out as a member of the parrot class. Basically red and white, the blooms are sometimes streaked with green. It grows 60cm/2ft tall and flowers in late spring.

between late summer and mid-autumn. Although catalogues often offer a more extensive range, their prices may be higher, so check available outlets before you buy.

Be sure to choose healthy

substitute and a little sand will do famously. Tulips must have good drainage if they are to overwinter in the soil.

Plant your bulbs with their noses pointing upwards in holes at least 15cm/6in deep. Do not risk planting them any deeper if your garden has a heavy clay soil.

Tulips look best in beds if they are gathered into bold groups. Place your bulbs at least 10cm/4in apart. Informality is easier to achieve if you plant in drifts or groups made up of odd numbers of bulbs.

Provide your tulips with some bone meal to aid root growth. Either give them a top dressing at a rate of 140g per sq m/4oz per sq yd or sprinkle a small handful at the base of each planting hole.

Tulips like a sunny position and will tolerate virtually any soil, although they prefer it on the alkaline side if possible.

'Greenland' (above) is a typical viridiflora hybrid, its open, pink and creamy-white flowers streaked with a band of rich green.

Plant tall or top heavy varieties, like the doubles, in a sheltered spot away from winds.

Small varieties look well when planted in a rockery, container or raised bed. Larger varieties will also grow happily in containers but are probably best used to provide spots or large drifts of colour in beds and borders.

After the show
Remove dead flower heads and allow the foliage to die back naturally. Deeply planted bulbs may be left in place unless your soil is heavy.

If you wish to lift your bulbs, wait until the foliage has died back completely before removing them and store them in a cool, dry place.

You can increase the number of plants you have by removing the offsets when you lift the bulbs for storage. Plant them in late autumn in a nursery bed at a depth of at least twice their size. The big ones may flower the following year, while smaller ones may take up to three years.

'Plaisir' (left) is a low-growing (15-20cm/6-8in) greigii hybrid, flowering in mid to late spring. Like all in its class, it has variegated foliage, its pale green leaves striped brownish-purple.

Hyacinths

Sweet-smelling hyacinths bring spring colour to the garden and can banish the drabness of winter from normally flowerless rooms.

Of all the spring bulbs, hyacinths are perhaps the most widely used for indoor cultivation, providing bold colour and a sweet, pervasive fragrance from Christmas to Easter when grown indoors in bowls or pots. But these versatile performers can also give fine displays in outdoor beds or in window-boxes and tubs through the spring. Indeed, they may start their lives as indoor plants, perhaps as Christmas gifts, and go on to give many years of pleasure in the garden.

For most people, the image of the hyacinth that will most immediately spring to mind is that of the tubular-flowered hybrids commonly known as Dutch hyacinths, varieties of *Hyacinthus orientalis*. This large bulb produces a single, heavily-scented flower spike 10-15cm/4-6in long. This spike is tightly packed with small, bell-shaped flowers.

Varieties of Dutch hyacinth can be purchased in a wide range of clear colours: its blooms may be white, cream, yellow, pink, red or blue. New varieties and shades appear every year.

Left to their own devices in the garden, Dutch hyacinths will flower from mid to late spring, although they can be persuaded to flower earlier indoors by a technique known as 'forcing'. Special, treated bulbs which can be forced into flower by Christmas are also widely

Hyacinths are famed for their sweet scent and vivid colour, especially shades of blue. H. 'Ostara' (right) verges on indigo.

PLANT PROFILE

Suitable site and soil Both Dutch hyacinths and grape hyacinths will grow in full sun or light shade, in well-drained soil.

Planting Plant Dutch hyacinths 15cm/6in deep in early to mid autumn. Grape hyacinths should be planted at the same time, but at half the depth.

Cultivation and care They need little care during the growing season except for water in dry spells. After flowering, remove dead blooms but leave the stalk intact. Leaves and flower stems should be left to wither and die naturally.

Propagation Prepare Dutch hyacinths by slitting the base of the bulb two or three times with a sharp knife in the autumn before planting. This encourages the growth of small offsets which may later be separated and planted out. Prepared bulbs cannot be propagated.

Grape hyacinths seed themselves rapidly: alternatively, lift and divide them every three years when the foliage has yellowed.

Pests and diseases Stem and bulb eelworm causes pale stripes on leaves, followed by twisted growth and deformed flowers and leaves. Infested bulbs are soft and may have a white woolly substance on the base. Healthy bulbs from reputable sources are usually grown in sterilized soil. Infested bulbs must be dug up and destroyed. Soft rot bacteria can occasionally attack pot-grown hyacinths. Flowers fail to develop and topple over at soil level while still in bud. This is precipitated by moist, humid conditions. Beware of over-watering.

Hyacinths are usually sold and planted in single colours. If you want a multi-coloured display in flower at the same time, buy a collection such as 'Multiflora Mixed' (above).

The Roman hyacinth (H. orientalis albulus) is smaller than the species but produces two or three headily fragrant, loosely packed, flower spikes. 'Rosalie' (right) is a good pink variety; others are blue or white. Dutch hyacinths such as the rich pink 'Jan Bos' (below) have a single, more compact spike.

available in garden centres.

A smaller subspecies, the Roman hyacinth (*H. orientalis albulus*) produces two or three flower spikes 15cm/6in high. These are thinner than those of the species, with fewer, more widely-spaced and stronger-scented white, pink or blue flowers. Like all hyacinths, it is frost hardy, but it does best when grown indoors and is the easiest of the varieties to force.

Outdoors, it will flower slightly earlier than the Dutch hyacinth; indoors, any time

from midwinter to early spring.

The very large-bulbed Multiflora hyacinth produces nine to twelve 15cm/6in flower stalks per bulb, with blooms in shades of white, pink or blue. Like the Roman hyacinth, it does best indoors, where it has the same flowering season.

Grape hyacinths

The smaller plants known as grape hyacinths belong to a different, but closely related genus of bulb, *Muscari*. However, with their tightly-packed flower spikes, they are suffi-ciently reminiscent of their larger cousin to merit their common name. In most species the petals of the individual flowers curve in, rather than out, giving them narrow mouths. Colours range from white through various shades of blue to a deep bluish purple which is almost black; only some species are fragrant.

Fast growers

Grape hyacinths are easy to grow and look their best in groups at the front of borders or as edging to mixed beds. They are also ideal rock garden plants and do well in tubs and window-boxes. The many different varieties can be seen in flower any time from early spring to midsummer.

Their only drawback is the speed with which they proliferate, especially *Muscari racemosum* syn. *Muscari neglectum*, which is really only suitable for wilder parts of the

Planting mixed colour schemes can be problematical because different varieties can flower a few days, even weeks, apart. Here (above), 'Delft Blue' is fully mature, while the white spikes of 'L'innocence' have yet to emerge completely from the green.

As with most Dutch hyacinths, the leaves of 'Pink Pearl' (above left) do not develop fully until after the plant has flowered.

'City of Haarlem' (left) has a distinct, pale yellow tint.

Varieties of the grape hyacinth Muscari armenaicum such as 'Blue Spike' (right) have a distinctive white fringe around the flower openings.

garden. With other species, divide and replant bulbs every three years after the leaves have turned yellow at the end of the growing season.

Rocky origins

The species form of *Hyacinthus orientalis*, which resembles the modern Roman hyacinth, is a native of western Asia, where it can be found growing amongst the rocks. The numerous wild varieties of grape hyacinths are also found in western Asia and the eastern Mediterranean.

GROWING TIPS

RECYCLING HOUSE PLANTS

After a forced hyacinth has flowered, remove the dead heads by running a hand up the stem from the base of the flower spike. Do not cut off the stalk. Continue watering until the leaves have withered and died down, then allow the compost to dry out, remove the bulbs and, having picked off any dried compost, dead roots or foliage, store in a cool, dry place until the autumn, when they may be planted out in the garden, with a little slow-acting fertilizer, such as bone meal, worked into the soil.

Bulbs grown in compost will often flower outdoors during their first spring, but those grown in bulb fibre will need more time to recover. Neither can be brought in and used again as houseplants.

FORCING

Hyacinths can be made to flower indoors from midwinter. Bulbs for forcing should be potted up at the end of the summer. They can be planted singly in 10-12cm/4-5in pots but look best when planted together in larger pots or bowls. Whatever you choose, make sure the bulb has room to develop roots. It is not a good idea to mix colours in containers as it is difficult to bring all of the colours into flower together.

In pots without drainage holes, a special bulb fibre should be used. For those with drainage holes, use a good potting compost – John Innes No. 1 or No. 2 would be fine.

Place a layer of moist compost or very moist (but not sodden) bulb fibre at the bottom of the container and set the bulbs on it, close together but not touching. Press them down very gently so that their bases are in firm contact with the compost. Making sure that they remain steadily upright, continue adding compost until the tops of the bulbs are just showing.

They now need about six to ten weeks of complete darkness in a temperature of not more than 5°C/40°F. Commercial growers bury them under peat until they are rooted and it is quite possible to do this at home, but it is just as effective to place the container in a black polythene bag and stand it in a cool corner of the garden. Check the bulbs occasionally to ensure the compost is still moist, but take care not to over-water.

When the shoot tips are around 2.5-5cm/1-2in high, bring the bowl indoors into a cool place (not more than 10°C/50°F), gradually increasing the amount of light and raising the temperature as the shoots grow larger.

As the leaves develop and flower buds appear, move the container to a bright, draught-free site around 15-20°C/60-70°F. Keep the compost moist at all times and turn the bowl occasionally to make sure you get even growth.

Far and away the most unusual plant in the hyacinth group is the tassel grape hyacinth (Muscari comosum 'Plumosum' syn. 'Monstrosum'), whose sterile flowers are superseded by a mass of purple threads (above). More conventionally shaped, but a startlingly clear white, is M. azureum album (left). The most vigorous member of the genus, though, is the deep blue M. neglectum syn. M. racemosum (right), which self-seeds rapidly and will soon take over a formal planting; it is best used in a semi-wild setting.

Hyacinths do not always suit companion planting. However, H. 'L'Innocence' is at home among the pink blooms of the low-growing double daisy Bellis perennis 'Rose Carpet'.

Given their origins, it is not surprising that both will flourish best in open, sunny situations with well-drained soil, although both will also tolerate partial shade, which will in fact extend their flowering period for a month or so.

Buying hyacinths

Dutch hyacinth bulbs are usually sold by size. For outdoor planting it is advisable to buy the smaller sized bulbs (16-17cm in circumference). The flower heads may not be as big, but they will be better able to withstand the squally weather of early spring.

For outside flowering, both hyacinth and grape hyacinth bulbs should be planted in early or mid autumn. Both look their best planted in small clumps rather than standing in rows like well-drilled soldiers, and both blend very well with daffodils.

Hyacinths should be planted to a depth of 15cm/6in and spaced 15-20cm/6-8in apart, and grape hyacinths to a depth of 8cm/3in, 10cm/4in apart. Some well-rotted compost or peat dug into the planting site a few days before planting will help to get your bulbs off to a good start.

HYACINTH JARS

Single hyacinths are often grown in glass bulb jars, which are sold in most gardening shops. The jar should be filled with water to a point just below the base of the bulb (*not* touching it). A small piece of charcoal in the bottom of the jar will help to keep the water fresh.

The jar should be kept in a cool, dark place until the roots are about 10cm/4in long and the leaves have begun to show, when it should be moved into a warmer and lighter spot.

Make sure the jar is kept topped up with water to the required level. Water-grown bulbs should be discarded at the end of their growing season as they will not flower again.

Begonias

The begonia family is vast and covers a huge spectrum of colours. With such a wide selection there is sure to be one to suit your garden.

Plants go in and out of fashion with every passing season and gardeners remain loyal to very few, but throughout the years the begonia has remained the queen of bedding plants – a favourite of experts and amateurs alike.

Outdoor types

Although the begonia family is large, most are grown as houseplants and only three types can realistically be used in the garden. These are wax begonias, also known as *B. semperflorens*, their newer cousins *B. hiemalis* (sometimes called Rieger hybrids) and tuberous begonias.

The Latin word *semperflorens* means 'always flowering'. Seen everywhere, in parks and

Begonias sold as Rieger hybrids, like the variety called 'Fireglow' (right), are developed from a type of begonia known as B.hiemalis. The vibrant orange flowers are larger and less fleshy than other types, and the button like yellow centre gives it a jaunty look.

You can guess from its showy blooms that the begonia (below) is tuberous – considered by many to be the most stunning member of the family. The pendulous types, like this 'Bridal Cascade', have slender, drooping stems.

public gardens, it is an easygoing plant which is happy in sun or shade and on any soil type as long as it is not waterlogged.

Wax begonias are half hardy but can be brought indoors before the frosts to go on flowering all winter. Available in pink, white and scarlet, they grow to a height of 15cm/6in, a good size for edging a border, for filling in spaces in rockeries or window boxes or for planting in pots to brighten up a patio or pathway.

Planted in a mass they may have a tendency to look rather

Tuberous begonias (right) last all summer and come in such vibrant colours that they will add a touch of sunshine even if it's raining. Use them in beds and borders or in containers. They are happy in sun or shade. Do not plant out until summer, however, as they do not like cold.

The wax begonia, B.semperflorens 'Thousand Wonders White' (right), has a simple charm which makes it quite irresistible. It flowers from early summer until late autumn and, if taken indoors, will go on flowering all through the winter.

institutional. For a prettier effect, pop them in here and there to provide spots of cheery colour.

Shopping choice

Buy this type of begonia from your local nursery or garden centre at the end of May, when you are sure the danger of late frosts is over, and plant them straight away.

Alternatively, you could order them in the depths of winter from a catalogue and they will be delivered as seedlings or 'plugs' at the appropriate time. It is easier to grow seedlings than to propagate your own plants from seed.

Bigger and better?

The plants generally sold as Rieger hybrids were developed from *B. hiemalis*. These have larger and more showy flowers than *B. semperflorens,* growing to a height of 25cm/10in.

They look splendid when grown in a patio pot but, although not as reliable as other types, they can be used in a border. When shopping for *B. hiemalis* look out for the Rieger hybrids, which are generally sold as house plants.

Loveliest of all, tuberous begonias come plain, frilled, or fringed, bi-coloured, pendulous and cascading. As they

WHICH WAY UP?

Tuberous begonias, whether trailing or not, must be planted hollow-side up. If you have trouble identifying one side from another, place the tubers in a polythene bag containing a few handfuls of moist compost, mix them around, then leave them in the airing cupboard or any warm, dark corner to develop roots.

Examine the tubers weekly. Little pink shoots will appear before any roots, so you will be able to tell which way up to plant them.

Some tuberous-rooted begonias, like the 'Nonstop' variety (below) can actually be grown from seed. They can also be bought as seedlings. An excellent variety for growing in containers, the radiant pink blooms look wonderful in this terracotta trough.

are so stunning it is best not to mix different types, though carefully selected colours — apricot, yellow and white, planted in a container — can look very effective.

Tuberous begonias

Buy tuberous begonias from garden centres, ready packed, complete with a colour photograph of the contents.

Look for fat, succulent tubers, some of which may already be sprouting. They should not be planted out until early summer. Until then you could start them off indoors but they will be perfectly safe in their packets. This type of begonia is happy in full sun but not in dry conditions, so make sure you keep them well watered.

Some of the tuberous-rooted begonias are now raised from

seed, and even if you do not have the facilities to raise seedlings yourself you can buy the plants from good garden centres in late spring and early summer. The 'Nonstop' range (as single colours or a mixture) are some of the best begonias for containers, beds

WELL FED

DON'T FORGET!

All begonias must be kept damp. Feed them at least once a week, while in flower, with a good proprietary mixture — but don't overfeed. Never apply liquid feed in bright sunlight or to dry soil.

and borders.

In late autumn, before the winter frosts begin, all begonias should be taken indoors. *B. semperflorens* will go on flowering in pots if you cut them back a little. Remove all the weak stems and water them very sparingly for the first few weeks. Feed them once they start flowering.

Winter care

Tuberous begonias must be allowed to die back to keep themselves fit for next year. Dig up the tubers gently, leaving a little soil on their roots, do not remove the stems. Store in trays in a frost-free place until the foliage has died right

down and the stems form part of the tuber.

The tubers should be covered in peat or an organic substitute. Peat has often been suggested in the past as the best medium in which to over-winter and then grow begonia tubers but there is a great deal of controversy about its use. The continued removal of peat poses a threat to wildlife.

Garden compost can be used just as successfully. Another alternative to peat is coir — a waste product from the coconut industry.

Whichever method you choose, make sure the tubers stay dry over the winter. You can then pot them up and start watering them lightly again in early spring when 'chits', which are like the little white sprouts you see on potatoes, should be appearing.

PERFECT PARTNERS

For a pretty contrast of shapes, combine a pink begonia with Fuchsia 'Thalia' in a complimentary shade.

Sunflowers

Sunflowers are one of our best loved old fashioned flowers. They bring a feeling of naturalness and simplicity that takes us straight back to the good life.

Old world cottages, hazy summer days, and the sort of romantic countryside scenes depicted in Victorian watercolours – these are the natural settings for sunflowers. But even if you live in town, sunflowers, with their strong nostalgic associations, somehow still conjure up those same images.

Quite apart from their country cottage image, sunflowers can be useful in all sorts of garden situations. A row of sunflowers makes a good, fast growing, but non-invasive temporary screen, ideal for creating privacy in summer when neighbours are out in their gardens, or when summer holiday traffic is at is heaviest.

A row of sunflowers also filters the breeze, giving you a pretty but effective shelter belt within which to sunbathe, or to grow more delicate flowers which would otherwise be spoilt by the wind.

Groups of tall sunflowers look good grown at the back of a tall herbaceous border, or among trees and shrubs to provide 'architectural interest'. And for wildlife gardens they are invaluable. A huge range of insects will visit the flowers, and if you leave the plants standing after the petals have dropped, you'll be able to enjoy hours of aerobatics as the birds swing upside down while they feed from the sunflower's springy-stemmed, seed-laden heads.

There is even something for floral artists, who like to cut a

few perfect seedheads and varnish them for winter decorations.

Famous for their golden, dinner plate sized flower heads and their tall stems, sunflowers are firm favourites with competitive growers – many villages organize giant

sunflower contests – and with schools for children's gardening projects, as well as ordinary gardeners in search of something spectacular.

There are perennial species, but the huge ones that most of us think of when sunflowers are mentioned are annuals.

The cottage garden is the traditional home of the sunflower, and there is no denying the appeal of a bunch of golden flower heads soaring out of a border (above). Here, the shape and colour of the flowers is echoed by the surrounding heleniums.

PLANT PROFILE

Suitable soil and site A sunny spot is essential for sunflowers. They will grow in any soil, but do best in rich, fertile soil that is reasonably well drained. Young plants can rot on cold, wet clay soil.

Propagation Sow seed in the garden where plants are to flower at the beginning of spring, choosing a mild spell of weather. Indoors, seed can be sown in pots from late winter on a warm, well lit window-sill.

Planting During mild, still weather in mid to late spring, when their pots have just filled with roots. Do not wait for them to become pot-bound. Knock plants out gently and tease a few roots out from the mass before planting. Plant to the same depth the sunflowers grew in

their pots – deep planting can encourage stems to rot.

Cultivation and care Once established, sunflowers are naturally quite drought resistant, but for several weeks after planting, water them during dry spells. For best results, feed once a week with general purpose liquid or soluble feed.

Pests and diseases Rarely a problem in mature plants, though seedlings are liable to rot in cold, wet, heavy clay soil or a sunless situation. Small seedlings may be smothered by weeds if the soil contains a lot of weed seeds; if this seems likely, sow sunflowers in pots on window-sills instead. Mature plants sometimes get greenfly, but these are soon cleared by birds such as blue tits.

Annual sunflowers come in a range of warm colours and tones. The fiery 'Autumn Beauty' (above) mimics the golden yellows and russet reds of autumn leaves, while 'Sunburst Mixed' (left) is a seed mixture that provides a profusion of colour. Neither of these varieties grows as tall as 'Giant Single' (below), which has a 30cm/1ft-diameter single yellow flower head carried aloft on a tall, thick stem.

Young plants are only rarely sold in garden centres, but there is usually a selection of seeds which are so quick and easy to grow at home that it's a shame to deprive yourself of the fun, even if bedding plants are available.

Start in winter or spring by choosing your seeds. Between them, the big seed firms list a good selection of sunflower varieties in their catalogues, which are available free of charge from late autumn onwards; just write and ask them to send you one.

This way, you'll be able to choose from a much bigger range of varieties than is normally available in garden centres. Don't worry about the Latin name; it is *Helianthus annuus*, but the seed is usually listed as sunflower.

Flower choice

The basic choices are between single and double flowers, between plain yellow flowers or one of the slightly more unusual shades such as bronze, orange, white, mahogany or even crimson, and between tall single stemmed plants or shorter bushier ones which

have more flowers, but of a smaller size.

For competition winning giant sunflowers, the variety to go for is 'Russian Giant' – one of the tallest sunflowers on record – which can grow to 2.5-3m/8-10ft or more. These are best grown against a wall, and ideally tied into place to keep them upright, especially if you want to grow a prize winner.

'Giant Single' is another tall one. At around 1.8m/6ft, it is

CHILDREN'S FAVOURITES

Young children find it difficult to sustain interest in gardening; things happen far too slowly for them. However, they are fascinated by the spectacular size and growth rate of sunflowers. The fact that they are so easy to grow makes them ideal plants for introducing young people to the joys of gardening. Encourage your child to join in when you plant and grow sunflowers, or set aside a section of a bed for their exclusive use.

BRIGHT IDEAS

RECOMMENDED VARIETIES

Russian Giant; single yellow flowers with yellow centres, 2.5-3m/8-10ft stems.

Giant Single; single yellow flowers with yellow centres, 1.8m/6ft stems.

Sungold; double orange-yellow flowers, 1.2-1.8m/4-6ft stems.

Orange Sun; deep orange double pompon flowers, 1m/3½ft stems.

Velvet Queen; medium sized single mahogany flowers with black centres, 1.5m/5ft stems.

Italian White; 10cm/4in wide creamy-white flowers with black centres, on 1.2m/4ft stems.

Sunburst Mixed; bushy sunflower with crimson, lemon, bronze and gold flowers zoned in contrasting colours on branching 1.2m/4ft tall stems.

Autumn Sunshine; yellow, bronze and red flowers, 1.2m/4ft stems.

Autumn Beauty; 15cm/6in wide lemon, gold, bronze and mahogany flowers with darker zones, strong 1.8m/6ft stems.

Sunspot; miniature sunflower with 20-25cm/8-10in wide single yellow flowers with yellow centres on 45cm/18in stems.

Teddy Bear; miniature sunflower with 15cm/6in wide double gold flowers on 60cm/2ft stems.

perfect for growing in rows as a tall screen or windbreak. Both varieties have single yellow flowers. And because all the plant's energies are concentrated into producing one huge flower at the top of that giant stem, the resulting flower heads are massive too.

Top doubles

If you fancy double flowers – highly spectacular creations, like huge, spiky orange or yellow pompons – then choose the orange-yellow 'Sungold', or 'Orange Sun', which has deep orange flowers.

If it's unusual shades you are after, try 'Velvet Queen' (mahogany with a black cen-tre), 'Italian White' (white, black centre), or one of the multicoloured seed mixtures available such as 'Sunburst Mixed' (crimson, lemon, bronze and gold, often attractively zoned in a contrasting colour), 'Autumn Sunshine' (yellow, bronze and red), or 'Autumn Beauty' (gold, lemon, bronze and mahogany).

These 'fancy' sunflowers are ideal for planting in borders with a mixture of other flowers. 'Sunburst Mixed', being a shorter, branching variety, rather than the traditional tall, upright sunflower, is particularly good grown in the middle of a border, where it looks rather like a sunflower bush, with flowers at the tips of all the shoots.

More unusual still, how about miniature sunflowers? Nowadays there are some truly knee-high ones, small enough to be grown in pots on the patio, or by the front door. 'Sunspot' is a real baby, just 45cm/18in tall. Most endearing of the lot is the 60cm/2ft tall 'Teddy Bear', which has cuddly double flowers of perfect teddy-bear gold.

Easy growth

Sunflowers are extremely easy to propagate. You can either sow seed straight into the garden, where you want the plants to flower, or grow them in pots on the window-sill and plant them outdoors when they are big enough.

Sowing straight into the garden is the best method for those short of time, since you only need to prepare the ground, sow and wait. Choose a sunny spot with good soil,

DON'T FORGET!

GOOD EATING

Sunflower seeds are a prized food source for all manner of wildlife. This can be a blessing in winter, when tits and other acrobatic birds flock in to pick the giant heads clean, but a curse in spring, when birds and mice scrabble up the seeds as soon as they are planted. To prevent any disappointment, sow far more seeds than you need.

The complex flowers of the Helianthus give way to extraordinary spiral-patterned seed heads (above left) that are often cut, varnished and used in winter displays by floral artists. They are also appreciated by birds, who perform aerial gymnastics to get at the oily, nutritious seeds.

Among the most charming of the dwarf sunflowers is the golden double 'Teddy Bear' (below), which grows to 60cm/2ft.

GARDEN NOTES

A SUNFLOWER SCREEN

Although it is an annual, the size of a sunflower and its habit of growing straight and tall makes it a good plant for temporary screening. A row of closely-planted sunflowers will make a windbreak or hide an unsightly shed while a more slow-growing perennial screening plant is getting established.

Taller varieties of Helianthus annuus are perfect for the back of the border, and make an excellent summer screen or windbreak, especially when the stems are tied into a trellis (above).

Though the larger varieties are best left in the garden, the smaller, bushier sunflowers can make an excellent, long-lasting cut flower (right).

and remove any weeds. Then fork in some organic matter (peat, coco-fibre, or well-rotted garden compost) and a handful of general purpose fertilizer. Sow the seeds 6mm/¼in deep and about 7.5cm/3in apart in late March or April. When they come through, thin them out, leaving the strongest seedlings spaced 30-90cm/1-3ft apart.

Growing on sills

Growing plants on a window-sill takes more attention, but produces earlier and better plants without risk of losses – and if you want sky-high plants, it gives them a longer growing season to get really tall. Sow three seeds per 9cm/3½in pot of seed compost in early March. Water in, and keep on a warm, well lit window sill, but out of bright direct sun to start with.

When the seeds start coming up, remove all but the strongest in each pot. Plant them out into well prepared soil when the plants fill their pots with roots (you will be able to see the roots escaping through the holes in the bottom of the pots).

Whichever way you grow your plants, sunflowers will do best if you keep them watered in dry weather, and feed them once a week with general purpose liquid feed. And with very tall varieties or in a windy area, tie sunflower stems to stakes to keep them upright.

Crocuses

Crocuses are among the cheeriest of plants, whose low-growing blooms bring swathes of colour to the garden from autumn to spring.

Crocuses have long been popular winter and spring flowers in gardens and parks. Their appeal lies in their range of buttery yellow, lilac to purple and white colouring. Some have deep throat markings, while others have markings like barley-sugar stripes on their outer surfaces.

The flowers look fragile and delicate close to, but massed clumps, especially when naturalized in a lawn, make a bold, sweeping statement.

Crocus leaves are long and thin, with a well-defined white stripe down the middle. *Crocus nudiflorus*, an autumn-flowering species, blooms before its leaves appear. It is also unusual among crocuses in that it spreads by underground stems, or stolons.

Most crocuses develop from small corms. Much of the long, tubular neck of the flower is below ground. The flowers respond to warmth on sunny spring days, opening to reveal cup-like faces with golden or orange stamens and stigmas.

The crocus story

Crocuses are hardy plants that belong to the iris family. They came to our gardens from the hilly areas of the eastern and northern Mediterranean, where they grow in wild profusion. There are about 70 species in all, with numerous varieties, including many garden hybrids.

The oldest cultivated crocus, saffron crocus (*C. sativus*), was introduced to many parts of Europe by the Romans. It is now rarely available, but was once grown as a crop around Saffron Walden in Essex.

In Spain and Kashmir, it is still grown commercially. Its intensely yellow stamens are used as a dye and a flavouring for sweets and savouries.

Many other crocuses were popular garden plants in Europe by the 16th century, and Dutch growers in the 18th and 19th centuries were famed for the hybrids they produced

from *C. vernus*. These hybrids, known as Dutch crocuses, flower in early spring, and have larger blooms than most other crocuses.

Small-flowered crocuses are hybrids of *C. chrysanthus*, many of them raised in the 20th century by the English plantsman, E. A. Bowles. They included a series named after

The winter-flowering crocuses first appear a month or so before the beginning of spring. Their petals and stamens bring to the garden a burst of rich, vibrant colour, positively startling after the muted hues of winter. This one (above) is C. tommasinianus *'Whitewall Purple'.*

PLANT PROFILE

Suitable site and soil Well-drained fertile soil in full sun. Dappled, light woodland shade is also suitable.

Planting Plant winter or autumn flowering crocus in late summer and spring crocus in autumn, 7.5cm/3in deep. Allow random spacing for best effect in lawns, under deciduous trees or in shrub borders, or plant 10cm/4in apart in a formal bed.

Cultivation and care Plant up crocus corms as soon as you get them. After flowering, allow foliage and flowers to die back naturally. Keep bulb sites well-watered in drought conditions, and especially during the growing seasons. If space is at a premium, lift and remove offsets every few years in autumn. Apply a sprinkling of fertilizer in autumn.

Propagation Tiny cormlets are produced. Lift clumps in the autumn, making sure to fork well under the clump to prevent damage. Remove offsets and dry them off in a warm shed or greenhouse, then clean off old skins, foliage, roots and old corms. Replant large offsets and they will probably flower the next season. Plant the smaller ones in straight rows to make weeding easier. In up to two years they will be large enough to plant in their flowering position. You can raise some species from seed but it takes up to four years and most garden hybrids will produce variable seedlings.

Pest and disease Mice and leatherjackets eat crocus corms. Deter mice with traps and fork a soil insecticide into the soil, especially in wet weather, to prevent leatherjacket attack. Prevent bird damage to spring flowers by making a network of black cotton across the flowering site. Corms in storage may be affected by dry rot and scab. Destroy affected corms and prevent infection by dipping corms in a fungal solution before storing them.

birds; 'Bullfinch', 'Yellow Hammer' and, still available today, 'Snow Bunting'.

Winter wonders

Crocuses can be divided in to three groups according to when they flower. Autumn crocuses, planted in late summer, bloom all through the autumn. They include the adaptable *C. speciosus* and its many gardens forms in white, deep purple and mauve. Its delicate petals are attractively marked with pale feather-like lines.

The basic crocus colour range includes shades of white, yellow and purple. Many of the garden varieties are single coloured, such as the golden yellow 'E.A. Bowles' (top), which is named after a famous gardener, and the lovely 'Cream Beauty' (above). Both of these are varieties of C. chrysanthus.

The species C. vernus (left) – here seen bursting its way characteristically through melting snows – is the parent of the numerous Dutch hybrid varieties.

RECOMMENDED VARIETIES

This selection from the wide variety of crocuses available is grouped according to flowering times. Many of the species are best obtained from specialist bulb producers.

Autumn
C. hadriaticus 'Tom Blanchard'. White with purple markings.
C. speciosus. Deep blue with veining.
C. nudiflorus. Pale mauve, leaves appearing later.
C. zonatus. Pale lilac with yellow centre.
Winter
C. imperati. Purple flowers with white and purple outer petals.
C. tommasinianus 'Whitewell Purple'. Purplish mauve flowers.
Spring
C. angustifolius. Golden yellow flowers with bronze veining.
Good *C. chrysanthus* hybrids include 'Cream Beauty'. Creamy yellow.
'E.A. Bowles'. Buttery yellow.
'Snow Bunting'. White inside with cream and lilac feathering on outside.
Dutch hybrid varieties (*C. vernus*) include
'Joan of Arc' (or 'Jeanne d'Arc'). White.
'Pickwick'. Striped.
'Enchantress'. Blue.
'Golden Mammoth.' Yellow
'Little Dorrit'. Lilac.

The tendency of some crocuses to have different colours on the inside and the outside of their petals, combined with the hybridizer's art, have created some unusual effects, such as the alternate blue and white petals of 'Bluebird' (above), or the contrasting shades of the heavily veined inner and outer petal surfaces of the Dutch hybrid 'Little Dorrit' (above right).

C. speciosus *(left) flowers in the autumn, while the new leaves do not appear until the end of winter. The open, heavily veined flowers are set off by divided golden stigmas.*

KEEP IT GREEN

Try to buy crocus corms from sources that you know cultivate the bulbs themselves or buy them in from other cultivators. Avoid buying where source is unknown since it is preferable not to deplete wild stocks for garden use.

done in the Netherlands, or as large-flowered crocuses.

They spread quickly, and look their best if allowed to naturalize in drifts of single colours. Their larger flower suits an informal, natural-looking planting. In a formal border or rockery they tend to look out of place and untidy.

They come in a wide colour range including white, pale shades of mauve, deep purple and golden yellow. There are also forms with striped markings on their outer petals.

Cloth of Gold crocus (*C. angustifolius*) has been delighting gardeners since the late 16th century. Its fragrant flowers have petal faces that

The winter-flowering group brighten the garden through the bleakest months. Their flowers are small, and they look very attractive grown on rockeries or naturalized in grass. The most dramatically coloured is *C. imperati*, with cream and purple striped outer petals and inner petals in a lovely, deep purple.

C. tommasinianus spreads speedily to make a starry show in shades of mauve and purple. First introduced to Britain in the 19th century, it was a great favourite in Victorian and Edwardian gardens.

The hybrids of *C. chrysanthus* are among the most widely available of all the winter-flowering crocuses, with a splendid variety of colours. Popular choices include 'Blue Bird', white inside with deep purple outer surfaces and a white edge to the petals, 'Cream Beauty', which has a soft and buttery yellow cup, and the lovely, deep yellow 'E. A. Bowles'.

Springing into action

Spring-flowering crocuses may also be described either as Dutch crocuses, as much of the work to produce them was

PLANTING CROCUSES

Crocuses may fail to flower if they are planted too deeply. Plant them just to twice their own depth, roughly 5-8cm/2-3in deep.

Do not worry about planting corms too shallow. They will adjust and pull themselves down to a depth to suit themselves.

PERFECT PARTNERS

Crocuses are the natural partners of other bulbs, such as daffodils. The best effects come from contrasting blocks of well-matched colour.

are a bright and sunny golden yellow, with bronzed, striped outer surfaces.

Buying crocuses

Buy and plant new corms as soon as they become available at garden centres or through mail order. If left in a warm place too long before planting, they will begin to deteriorate.

If you are buying direct from a garden centre, look the bulbs over carefully and discard all those which show any signs of damage or disease.

The brown covering of the crocus corm, the tunic, should be intact and in good condition. If the tunic is cracked or mouldy, discard the corm.

A sure sign of vigour is the

Generally, it is better to plant similarly coloured crocuses together rather than mixing different varieties. The exception to this rule is when they are naturalized in a lawn or scattered through a semi-woodland setting (below).

GROWING TIPS

THE NATURAL LOOK

Allow leaves of naturalized crocuses to die down before you mow the grass. Once flowering is over the leaves continue to grow and provide nutrition for next year's corm.

condition of the little white shoots that show on the top of the corm. If they look healthy, you are sure to have a good display of flowers.

By choosing from all three groups of crocuses you can fill your garden with a succession of colour from autumn through to spring, broken only for a few weeks in deep mid winter. Plant them in containers to brighten the patio. Site a patch of winter-flowering crocus to naturalize where you can see it from the house on gloomy days.

Although mixed colours can be pleasing, crocuses look more attractive when grouped in single colours. Where you are naturalizing them, allow the colour blocks to blend into each other.

There is no need to lift crocuses annually, but on a rockery or a border you may wish to dig up and divide clumps that are too crowded.

DON'T FORGET!

FALSE IDENTITY

Also flowering in autumn and commonly called autumn crocus, *Colchicum autumnale* is not a crocus. It belongs to the lily family. You can tell the difference by comparing the plants' corms. That of the crocus is neat and compact while the colchicum is very large indeed.

The flowers look very similar, but again, the purple, pink or white colchicum is bigger, with a fuller flower shape.

The winter-flowering C. imperati (right), with its striking two-tone petals is unusual in having a distinct, pleasant fragrance.

Geraniums

True geraniums are not as well-known as bedding geraniums – pelargoniums – but their delightful flowers and foliage earn them a place in anyone's garden.

It is easy to get confused about geraniums; the name is given to two completely different groups of plants. The group that most people think of as geraniums are, in fact, impostors. The handsome red, pink and white flowers that look so well in pots, window boxes and hanging baskets, are pelargoniums.

To distinguish them from true geraniums, some call pelargoniums 'bedding geraniums'. Like other bedding plants, they are not hardy and must be replaced annually or over-wintered indoors.

True geraniums – members of the *Geranium* genus – are perennials that bear only a superficial resemblance to the tender, bedding type. Some books and catalogues refer to them as cranesbills or hardy geraniums. The name cranesbill comes from the long

Geranium psilostemon syn. G. armenum (above) is an excellent all-rounder. Its single flowers, a vibrant magenta with a dark centre, provide mid-summer drama and the divided leaves colour well in the autumn.

PLANT PROFILE

Suitable site and soil Will grow in most soils but will not tolerate being waterlogged. One or two require alpine conditions because they cannot stand winter wet. Most prefer full sun but others thrive in deep or partial shade.

Planting Plant in well-drained soil, preferably in early spring or autumn, although container grown plants may be planted at any time.

Cultivation and care Dead head regularly during the flowering season to promote continuous blooming. Cut back tall varieties in autumn to encourage new growth from the base.

Propagation By semi-ripe cuttings in summer, by seed in early spring or by division in autumn. Hybrid varieties are best propagated by cuttings or division as they are unlikely to come true from seed.

Pests and diseases These sturdy plants are not particularly prone to attack from the usual pests such as slugs, snails and aphids. New, tender growth may possibly get some unwanted attention from slugs if there is nothing tastier on offer. Powdery mildew may cause problems if conditions are very dry in spring or if the planting site is robbed of moisture by tree roots. Use a proprietary fungicide. If you wish to avoid the use of chemicals, remove and destroy the infected leaves at the first sign of trouble and move the plant to a more suitable site.

curved 'beak' of the seed pods.

Their shallow, cup-shaped flowers come in clear, jewel-bright shades of pink, mauve, purple or blue. Crisp whites are also available.

In some varieties, the foliage brings an added interest. Geraniums often have delicate, deeply divided leaves, attractive in their own right. There are evergreen varieties and a few that offer autumn colour when their leaves turn a glorious red or bronze. Some have aromatic foliage.

Friendly plants

Most cranesbills are fully hardy and will give you years of pleasure. A few do fall into the half hardy category, so check for hardiness before you buy.

They are easy to get along with as, once planted, they tend to require very little attention from you; they are not particularly prone to pests and diseases and require little or no mollycoddling. Regular dead-heading will ensure a continuous show of charming, jaunty flowers for a long period in summer.

The only condition that geraniums will not tolerate is waterlogged soil. Some like things on the dry side, others prefer more moisture, but all require decent drainage. They will, therefore, thrive in virtually any soil except unimproved heavy clay.

Although most geraniums like a sunny position, there are some that come in handy for more troublesome spots such as deeply shaded areas.

The glossy-leaved *G. nodosum* is one such plant, with delicate, cup-shaped flowers in tones of lilac pink to bring cheer to dark corners.

Another shade-lover is *G. phaeum*, whose soft green leaves and sombre maroon-

The muted colours and bowed heads of the shade-loving G. phaeum (above) have given rise to its common name, mourning widow.

The two-toned 'Buxton's Blue', also known as 'Buxton's Variety' (below), is the only commonly available variety of G. wallichianum.

Vigorous and long-flowering, G. 'Johnson's Blue' (above) is an excellent, clump-forming border plant.

The species form of bloody cranesbill (G. sanguineum) is veined with red, but the subspecies lancastrense (below) is a more anemic hue, with dark pink veins.

purple flowers give rise to its rather sad common name of mourning widow.

Partial or dappled shade suits some geraniums best. *G. sylvaticum* 'Mayflower' is one candidate for such a position. Its cup-shaped flowers are a lovely violet-blue with white centres. *G. wallichianum* 'Buxton Blue', also known as 'Buxton's Variety', is a much paler blue, and its pretty white centre gives it a delicate air. It flowers from midsummer but is at its best a little later, when it gives a bright, fresh touch to the autumn tones surrounding it.

True grit

Some compact geraniums are at their best in rock gardens, alpine beds, sinks or scree gardens, where they appreciate the good drainage provided.

They have the added advantage of flowering in summer, when many alpines are past their best. *G. dalmaticum* is an excellent choice; it will drape itself elegantly over the edge of an alpine sink in no time at all. It has pretty, shell-pink flowers over dark green, divided leaves. The foliage provides winter interest as it is evergreen except in the harshest of conditions.

G. cinereum 'Ballerina' is a purplish-pink form which has lovely deep purple veins, while a subspecies, *G. c. subcaulescens*, has the most glorious magenta blooms. Both of these

SILVER LINING

The deep pink, purple, blue or magenta varieties of hardy geraniums look particularly handsome with silver-foliaged plants.

Lavandula spica 'Vera' or 'Hidcote' are a good choice because they bring a lovely fragrance. Their flower spikes contrast well with the softer looking blooms of geraniums.

Tanacetum haradjanii has pretty, feather-like, grey leaves that make a perfect foil for deep coloured geraniums. Rich pinks look good with it too. Remove the flowers as they appear as they tend to detract from the foliage.

Various members of the *Dianthus* family can be a good choice. Check that the flower colours are complementary before buying.

With its low-growing habit and densely-packed, aromatic, semi-evergreen foliage, G. macrorrhizum (above) is a good weed-suppressing ground-cover plant; the same qualities allow it, as here, to tumble attractively over and down a low wall.

The meadow cranesbill (G. pratense) has a lovely, intensely coloured double form (left) which is known variously as 'Flore Pleno' and 'Plenum Violaceum'.

G. cinereum is an alpine species which rarely exceeds 15cm/ 6in in height. The purple-veined variety 'Ballerina' (right) is even smaller, just 10cm/4in tall.

PERFECT PARTNERS

The carpeting habit of many geraniums makes them a suitable choice for 'filling in' shrub beds. Here, *G. pratense* 'Kashmir White' combines beautifully with *Rosa* 'Aloha'.

are suitable for rock gardens although they will also thrive in a well-drained border.

Bed and border

Geraniums make fine subjects for sunny herbaceous beds and borders, where they are useful as well as beautiful. Low, spreading varieties are ideal for softening the hard edges of paths, while taller varieties fill the gap between low growing, front-of-border plants and the giants at the rear.

Several varieties are excellent for the middle of a border. *G.* 'Johnson's Blue' for instance, will flower all summer long, bringing continuity of form and clear blue colour. It grows to a height of 30cm/1ft and a spread of 60cm/2ft.

The long flowering period of geraniums helps to keep things going in a border, filling the awkward gaps between spring and summer bloomers and between summer flowers and autumn colour.

Several varieties of geranium have foliage which gives good autumn colour and soft-coloured flowers which are invaluable when used as buffers between more dramatic plants that would otherwise make uneasy bedfellows.

G. psilostemon, also known as *G. armenum*, has a height and spread of 1.2m/4ft, so it needs plenty of room to display its magenta flowers with dramatic black centres and rich autumn tints. This handsome variety makes a good foil for silver-leaved plants.

The meadow cranesbill (*G. pratense*) can be invasive, spreading itself freely through the garden, but there are several suitable garden varieties, such as 'Kashmir White', 'Kashmir Purple' – these two are sometimes listed as *G. clarkei* – and the blue double 'Flore Pleno'.

Cover stars

Some varieties can be useful for providing attractive ground-cover. Their masses of handsome foliage will save you hours of work by smothering potential weeds before they can colonize your bed or border. *G. macrorrhizum* is an excellent choice for this job. It makes a low-spreading carpet of aromatic leaves and has clusters of pale pink or soft magenta flowers.

The bloody cranesbill (*G. sanguineum*) forms lovely hummocks of deeply divided, dark green leaves, crowned in summer with masses of beautiful, cup-shaped, deep magenta flowers.

Perhaps the most popular, and certainly one of the most widely available ground cover geraniums is *G. endressii* 'Wargrave Pink', with a dense habit and salmon pink flowers through the summer.

A spreading habit is also handy for bridging large gaps between shrubs. Geraniums with glowing magenta flowers make handsome, undemanding companion plants in a bed of old roses, for example.

Ivy

Ivy is one of the most versatile evergreen garden plants, providing a range of foliage shapes, colours and textures to set off its autumn flowers and fruits.

Ivy's natural tendency to creep and climb make it a perfect choice for ground cover or to clothe a wall or shed. Its long trailing shoots are particularly pleasing tumbling from window boxes or hanging baskets. It is also much enjoyed as an indoor plant.

Ivy is a woody perennial plant that can live for many hundreds of years. It has two distinct phases of growth. Young or juvenile ivy, with deeply indented or lobed leaves, is most commonly found in gardens. It scrambles along the ground or climbs, using small aerial roots that grow from its stems to anchor it to supports.

The next phase in its growth, when it has reached sufficient height and light, is to develop slightly oval, entire leaves. The stems become thicker and no aerial roots are present. In autumn, the plant produces umbels of tiny, greeny-white flowers, followed by black berries.

This mature form, known as tree or arborescent ivy, can be grown as an independent shrub or allowed to continue growing as a scrambling plant, making dense cover on trees and walls.

There are seven species of

Hedera helix 'Buttercup', H. colchica and H. canariensis 'Variegata' (above) combine to make an attractive, dense wall cover.

All ivies produce small black fruits in autumn (above right) with the exception of H. helix 'Poetica' which bears glorious yellow berries.

One of the most popular climbers is the delightful H. helix 'Goldheart' (right), with its splashy yellow centres.

ivy, including common ivy (*Hedera helix*), which has over 300 varieties. Varieties of common ivy can themselves be divided into groups. Ivies that produce long, unbranched trails are described as vining, and are best used as climbers. The second group, self-branching ivies, produce branching shoots along the main stems, and are suitable for ground cover and for growing in containers both indoors and outside.

Uncommonly versatile

Common ivy, a favourite for use in seasonal festive door wreaths, is one of the best choices for glossy, evergreen ground and wall cover. It quickly covers unsightly tree stumps and lends an air of romantic antiquity to corners

PLANT PROFILE

Suitable site and soil Ivy's woodland origin is a guide to the site and soil in which it thrives; partial shade, with a cool root run under a mulch of leaves or compost. Ivies with variegated leaves need more light and may be less hardy in severe conditions. All ivies grow best in well-drained fertile soils.

Planting Plant container-grown ivies at any time, although spring and autumn are generally best. Dig a hole larger than the root-ball, water well and add well-rotted organic matter or a handful of bone meal. Spread roots out into the hole, and firm the plant in.

Cultivation and care Water thoroughly in dry conditions. If growing ivy against a wall or other support, tie in the longest shoots to encourage climbing. Apply liquid fertilizer in the growing period. Trim from time to time to encourage new growth. Variegated and coloured leaf ivies do not respond well to regular trimming.

All ivies can be cut back once they have reached the desired height and spread. Cut out any shoots that revert to green on variegated plants and, if you do not want the mature tree ivy form to develop, cut this out, too, as it appears.

Propagation Take cuttings from new growth from early summer through to autumn. Each cutting should have at least three leaves. Remove the lower leaf and pot up to just below the leaf node. Use a well-draining mixture of sand and two parts peat for cuttings.

Insert the cuttings around the edge of a 9cm/3½in pot and cover with a plastic bag. Keep in a humid place out of direct sun for three weeks.

Alternatively, layer ivy stems on the ground or into pots. It will be at least four weeks before you can cut new ivy from the parent plant.

Pests and diseases Mainly trouble free, but in hot, dry conditions red spider mite is likely. Scale insects and aphids are found on indoor and wall-grown ivies. Leaf spot and powdery mildew may occur in damp conditions.

where it is allowed to scramble and climb freely.

In dense shade, under trees, where little else would grow satisfactorily, common ivy will provide a glimmering green cover to suppress most tough annual weeds.

Ivy is also one of the most popular indoor plants, known for its ability to tolerate low light levels and any amount of neglect. Recently it has acquired a reputation as a purifer of polluted office air. Its attractive foliage has long been popular for the way it softens and warms interiors.

As a wall plant, ivy is very accommodating, as it does best on difficult north, east or west

Hedera helix 'Glacier' (right) is a favourite ground-cover ivy. It is notably hardy and its variegated silver-grey leaves are particularly attractive.

The romantic associations of the heart-shaped leaves of H. helix 'Deltoidea' (far right), combined with its stiff stems, make it a popular choice for flower arrangers.

H. colchica 'Sulphur Heart' (below right) is equally at home as a climber or as ground cover. Its large variegated leaves have a central splash of colour.

walls, leaving precious south-facing walls free for more sun-loving climbers.

It is usually quite slow growing in its first year, but once settled it will race ahead. It may need tying in or staking to encourage it in the direction you wish it to climb. Some of the larger-leaved ivies are too heavy to support themselves, and will need a permanent support system.

A large canvas

This may be a practical disadvantage, but in decorative terms means you can provide colour and cover on the same scale as a big wall surface. Persian ivy (*Hedera colchica*), with its wide, almost handkerchief-shaped leaves, suits such a large canvas. The variety 'Dentata' (elephant's ears), and its variegated forms 'Dentata Variegata' and 'Sulphur Heart', need support to

RECOMMENDED VARIETIES

Climbers

Hedera azorica 'Typica' is very hardy, fast-growing with large matt green leaves.

H. canariensis 'Gloire de Marengo' (also sold as 'Variegata') is fast-growing. Has creamy-white edges to its elegant leaves.

H. colchica 'Dentata' has large, unlobed leaves. Its variegated forms, 'Dentata Variegata' and 'Sulphur Heart', have attractive colouring and are good climbers, but need supporting.

Hedera helix 'Buttercup' needs a sunny position. 'Glymii' is dark purple in winter and a good climber. 'Goldheart', with green edges to its golden-centred leaves, is a hardy climber that needs no support.

Ground cover

'Glacier' has silver-grey foliage. Hardy and good indoors as well. 'Brokamp' has willow-like, medium-sized leaves. One of the few ivies to remain bright green in winter. 'Deltoidea' has heart-shaped leaves that turn to bronze in winter.

Containers

'Kolibri' has white speckled leaves and trails prottily. 'Adam' has creamy-white leaf edges that turn to pink in winter. 'Midas Touch' has wavy golden variegation and needs a sheltered position. 'Poetica' is a very old ivy, grown mostly as a mature tree ivy for its yellow berries. Grow it in a container for a few years then plant it out as a specimen shrub.

low leaves, are less hardy. In severe winters they will be damaged by wind and frost, though the plants will survive.

For best colouring, plant variegated ivy such as 'Glacier', 'Anne Marie' or 'Chester' where it gets good dappled sunlight. For green ground cover, choose 'Dragon Claw', with its deeply waved leaves, or 'Brokamp', which has light green angular foliage.

Useful as a climber or trail-

ing from a container, sweetheart ivy (*H. helix* 'Deltoidea') is undoubtedly best as a ground cover plant. Its dark green, almost heart-shaped leaves deepen to a purplish hue in winter. Its rather stiff stems make it a popular choice for flower arrangers.

Ivy contained

Cascades of delicate, smaller-leaved green and variegated ivy trailing from hanging bas-

start but once growing well will provide a generous splash of colour and shine to lighten a bare wall.

For well-defined, bright pools of sunlight yellow on a north facing wall, use *H. helix* 'Goldheart', whose green-edged leaves have a strong yellow centre. The sunniest of all ivies, the beautiful 'Buttercup', needs full sun to perform at its best, producing marble-textured, entirely yellow leaves, although young plants are likely to be green.

On the level

There are both green and variegated ivies suitable for ground cover, but variegated ivies, especially those with yel-

PERFECT PARTNERS

Hedera helix 'Buttercup' can make a wonderful backdrop for climbing flowers but few combinations are as happy as this one, interwoven with the pretty *Rosa* 'Bantry Bay'.

kets and window boxes can provide year-round pleasure. Whether they are used with annual summer plants or with spring bulbs, ivies offer an exuberant show, softening and adding line and texture to container displays.

There are many varieties to choose from, including 'Kolibri' with its white speckled leaves. It is equally at home grown in containers in or outside. 'Adam' with creamy-white leaf edges that turn pinkish in winter, looks attractive trailing from terracotta urns or window boxes. 'Midas Touch' with its golden variegation can make a very rich splash of colour, given a sheltered position. For unusually shaped green leaves, use 'Fluffy Ruffles' or 'Manda's Crested'.

In winter the leaves of some ivies deepen from green to bronze, while others turn a rich purple. 'Atropurpurea' (also known as 'Purpurea') and 'Glymii', both good climbing plants, turn a deep purple, while 'Succinata', which has been grown since the 1800s, has bronzed leaves in winter and amber spring growth.

Buy small plants rather

than large, well-established plants for climbing. Only new growth will cling to supports and wall surfaces and young plants will establish quicker.

To cover a large wall you will need to put your plants about 90cm/3ft apart. For good ground cover you will need one plant for every square metre or square yard.

Looking after ivy

Ivies grow in most soil conditions, but do best if the ground is not heavy. Prepare it by forking it over well and adding well-rotted organic matter. A well-drained soil makes it easier for ivy's deep soil roots to find the necessary nutrients for growth.

As an alternative to adding bulky organic matter, when planting put a slow-release fertilizer on the base of the planting hole.

Although ivy will compete successfully with most annual weeds, give it a good start and remove them from the planting area. Remove perennial weeds too, as ivy will not be able to suppress them.

Water the new plants in and in dry conditions ensure they are well watered until they settle down. Cover the soil around the plants with a leaf-mould or bark mulch. Ivy in containers must be kept well watered, but, once established, ivy in the ground will be fairly drought resistant.

In spring, scatter granular fertilizer around established plants. Cut out any green shoots on variegated ivies and trim back green ivies when they need controlling.

H. helix 'Manda's Crested' (below) used to be called 'Curly Locks' which describes it well. It can make an attractive container plant or be used as ground cover.

The trailing habit of the speckled, white, variegated ivy, H. helix 'Kolibri' (bottom), makes it a charming plant for hanging baskets or pots.

Holly

The scarlet berries and glossy, prickly leaves of holly are synonymous with Christmas, but the holly family has many garden uses beyond the festive season.

The shimmering green foliage and bright red berries of common holly (*Ilex aquifolium*) are a traditional display for the winter garden. There are, however, many other species and varieties to choose from in the *Ilex* genus which will provide extra-special leaves and berries.

Not all hollies have plain green foliage. Many have leaves with creamy-gold or silvery edges or centres that turn a mature plant into a warm and glowing block of colour. Some species are deciduous, though most are evergreen.

Holly leaves also vary in prickle. The spiniest of them all, hedgehog holly (*Ilex aquifolium* 'Ferox'), a male plant, has purplish spring shoots and spines all over the leaf surfaces as well as the edges, while others are totally smooth all round.

As well as the usual scarlet, holly berries can be deep red, orange, yellow and even black.

To enjoy the winter charms of holly best, many people plant it close to the house. Perhaps they know that our ancestors planted holly near the front door to protect the home from lightning strikes!

Garden hollies

Common holly (*Ilex aquifolium*) has many varieties making bushy trees that, if left to grow unchecked, can reach up to 20m/65ft. Also available in many forms, resistant to pollu-

Edged with frost, holly leaves and berries reveal their winter charm. A traditional festive decoration since pagan times, holly is believed to have life-giving qualities and to be a symbol of good luck.

tion and frost hardy, is *I.* × *altaclarensis*. It is shorter than common holly and makes a tapering, pyramidal shape. These two provide most of our common garden varieties of holly, though some other species can also be grown.

Box-leaved or Japanese holly (*I. crenata*) for example, will eventually grow up to 4.5m/ 15ft, but is slow-growing and useful in containers.

Winterberry (*Ilex verticillata*) is a deciduous shrub with suckering stems that grow from the base of the plant. Its otherwise bare autumn stems are crowded with bright berries that will provide colour all through the winter.

A question of sex

Holly plants take some years before they establish themselves happily in a garden and begin flowering. To be sure of colourful berries for future festive decorations you will need to have both a male and a female plant; most varieties of holly are unisexual.

There is no need to worry if space is limited, as there are two exceptions that are self-fertile. *I. aquifolium* 'J.C. van Tol' and 'Pyramidalis' both produce an abundance of red berries all by themselves.

Both male and female holly plants bear tiny, white spring flowers. If you are not sure whether an established holly is male or female, closely examine the flowers. If they have a round centre they are fe-

male. Male flowers have stamens with pollen.

Holly makes a dense animal and burglar-proof hedge. Here you can use plain green holly or one of the many variegated hollies to make a light and glowing boundary.

Plant *I. aquifolium* 'Handsworth New Silver', a female with cream-edged green leaves, in combination with at least one 'Silver Queen' – male despite the name – to ensure plenty of bright red berries in winter. One male plant will be sufficient to fertilize many females. For a long boundary hedge you need to include just one male for every 24 plants.

Space the plants 45cm/18in apart, and trim them with secateurs in midsummer. When the plants have reached the height you require, trim their tops as well as the sides.

Holly borders

Holly can be a very effective plant in a mixed shrub border. Even plain green holly pro-

vides a glossy, evergreen background for other shrubs.

Variegated varieties need a position in full sun, but repay you with added colour. For strong golden-yellow variegation choose from *I. aquifolium* 'Golden Milkboy' (male), 'Golden Queen' (male), 'Madame Briot' (female) and 'Golden van Tol' (female).

'Handsworth New Silver' (female) is a good all round holly for the smaller garden. It has creamy leaf margins and bears a profusion of berries. Use it for hedging or as a spe-

The hedgehog holly is the prickliest of all hollies, with spines over the entire leaf surface. This variety (above), Ilex aquifolium 'Ferox Argentea', is attractively edged with cream margins.

The deciduous Ilex verticillata, known as winterberry (above right), has saw-toothed, bright green leaves, but is best known for its long-lasting bright red berries, which remain on bare branches right through the winter.

I. aquifolium 'Pyramidalis' (above far right) is self-fertile and produces abundant red berries. Growing to only 6m/20ft, it is particularly suitable for a small garden.

Japanese holly (I. crenata) is useful for landscaping or for hedging. The dwarf variety 'Golden Gem' (right), with golden-yellow leaves, can make a good container plant.

RECOMMENDED VARIETIES

Ilex aquifolium has glossy green leaves with prickles. It has an upright shape and can grow to 20m/65ft. Females produce red berries if a male is present.

'J.C. van Tol' has dark green, slightly spiny leaves. Self-fertile, it produces abundant red berries. Grow it as a specimen, in a container or as a hedge plant.

'Argentea Marginata' (female) has dark green leaves with silvery margins. New leaves are a lovely pink in spring. Grows in a columnar shape.

'Handsworth New Silver' (female) also has a columnar shape and creamy-edged, fairly prickly leaves, but is a good holly for a small space.

'Pyramidalis' is self-fertile and grows to 6m/20ft. Its leaves are slightly spiny and green. Abundant red berries.

'Amber' (female) produces orange berries.

'Pyramidalis Fructu Luteo' has green leaves and clusters of yellow berries.

'Flavescens' or moonlight holly (female) has dark green leaves flushed with yellow when young. Needs good light and reaches 6m/20ft.

'Golden Queen' (male) has a dense, oval shape. Its green leaves are edged with yellow.

'Madame Briot' (female) has gold-edged leaves and produces deep red berries.

I × altaclarensis 'Golden King' (female) has new growth flushed with purple and leaves edged with yellowy-cream. It does not fruit well but makes a lovely specimen plant.

'Wilsonii' (female) has spiny green leaves and produces deep red berries. Grow it as a hedge plant.

'Camelliifolia' (female) grows in a pyramid shape to make a very strong, architectural specimen tree. It produces large, deep red fruits and has very glossy, smooth leaves.

cimen plant in a lawn.

Hollies are slow-growing, so specimen plants look a little lost for a while in a sea of lawn. Once they get going they become quite stately, although you can keep their height in check by pruning if you wish.

PERFECT PARTNERS

Variegated holly and the miniature bush rose, *Rosa* 'Baby Masquerade', can make an effective summer-autumn display, with holly berries adding colour as the roses fade.

One drawback, though, is that evergreen hollies shed some old leaves in early summer. Once they have been blown around the garden they can crop up painfully if they get into soil where you are weeding. To avoid this, grow relatively smooth-leaved hollies such as *I. × altaclarensis* 'Camelliifolia' or 'Golden King'. Both these handsome plants are females, so you will need a male somewhere nearby if they are to produce a crop of berries.

For smooth leaves and good shape, grow one of the self-fertile holly varieties, 'J.C. van Tol' or 'Pyramidalis'.

Berried treasure

Red is the colour associated with holly's berries, but there are many colours to discover. For beautiful bright yellow berries, plant *I. aquifolium* 'Bacciflava' or 'Pyramidalis Fructu Luteo'.

For orange berries choose 'Amber', and for black berries,

the Japanese holly (*Ilex crenata*) and its forms 'Convexa' and 'Helleri'. The spreading growth of these low-growing, black berried hollies suits landscape plantings, helping to soften lines at the edges of houses and patios, and also makes a good hedge.

Containing holly

For a patio tub choose one of the box-leaved hollies, such as *I. crenata* 'Golden Gem' with yellow-green leaves.

I. aquifolium 'Silver Queen' (male), with its silver-edged leaves, also does well in a container, where the pink lustre of its new shoots and spring

The male and female hollies (above), I. aquifolium 'Golden Queen' (left) and I. altaclarensis 'Golden King' (right) are most confusingly named; the former is male and the latter, female.

I. aquifolium 'Amber' (above right) is one of the most glorious hollies, producing vibrant orange berries for striking winter colour.

I. aquifolium 'Handsworth New Silver' (right) has prickly green leaves with attractive cream margins. It makes a good hedge or specimen plant and is suitable for small gardens.

leaves can best be appreciated in a position close to the house.

Make sure the container has a good drainage layer and fill it with a loam-based compost. Keep the plant well-watered until it is established. After that it will still need watering regularly, but less often.

Buy container-grown hollies and get them planted quickly as root disturbance sets the plants back. For best variegation and berry production grow holly in a sunny position.

Plant in well-drained gar-den soil in spring or autumn. Water young plants well throughout the growing sea-son so that they establish quickly. Variegated plants are slower than green hollies, but once they are established they will grow well.

In winter, protect young plants from drying, freezing winds. Prune out any dead or damaged wood in spring. Keep hedges in trim in late summer, and in early winter make a pre-festive season pruning to use as indoor decorations.

Aquilegias

The dainty columbine is one of Britain's loveliest wild flowers, and its hybrid forms add grace and summer colour to many areas of the garden.

Aquilegias are graceful perennial plants, much loved by generations of cottage gardeners. They enjoy several appealing traditional names; columbine because the flowers reminded our ancestors of a gathering of doves, and 'granny's bonnets' for reasons that are obvious the moment you set eyes on the delightful, jaunty flowers.

There are many reasons why aquilegias have enjoyed an enduring popularity, but the main one is that they manage to combine exquisite delicacy of form with an easy going temperament and an admirable robustness.

Short but sweet

Although aquilegias are perennial, their life span may be fairly brief. However, what they lack in longevity they more than make up for in their exquisite beauty.

Their graceful and intricate flowers are borne on slender stems which rise out of rosettes of delicate, fern-like foliage. The blooms themselves come in a range of colours from rich, dark blue, crimson and purple to pastel shades of pink, cream, white, yellow, blue and violet. Modern hybrids are often bi-coloured. All forms have distinctive spurs behind their petals, which vary in length depending on which variety you select.

Free and easy

Aquilegias are very obliging and will self-sow with enthusiasm. This is fine as long as you do not mind hybrids reverting to their native forms, which can be very pretty, and

The wild columbine (Aquilegia vulgaris) is the ancestor of many of today's garden hybrids. The pert, yet dainty flowers, which have earned it the name of granny's bonnets, can be found in various tones of white, pink, blue and purple *(above)*.

A. flabellata (left) is smaller than most garden aquilegias, forming clumps just 25cm/10in high. Its natural habitat is woodland, so it positively enjoys a moist, shady site, and makes an excellent subject for a container on a patio out of full sun.

The distinctive 'Nora Barlow' (left) is one of the most popular of all garden hybrids, and will sometimes come true to seed. It bears handsome, double, bi-coloured flowers above a mound of soft, grey-green leaves and, like its parent species, A. vulgaris, grows to 90cm/3ft tall.

The alpine columbine (A. alpina) is a much smaller plant, growing to just 30cm/1ft (below). It makes a good rockery subject, but can also, as here, make an effective statement when several plants are grouped informally at the edge of a border.

tend to be daintier than their highly bred relatives. Very few types will come true to seed, although *A. vulgaris* 'Nora Barlow' is occasionally an exception to this rule.

Cross-pollination is rife among aquilegias; therefore, if you wish your stocks to remain pure-bred, it is a good idea to keep separate varieties well away from each other. If, on the other hand, you quite like surprises, mix them all up together, collect their seeds at the end of the season and either plant them in trays or scatter them where you wish them to flower. It can be exciting to see what comes up.

Aquilegias look wonderful anywhere in the garden and even when they are not flowering, their handsome foliage is useful for filling in gaps. Most varieties enjoy a site in full sun, but they will tolerate a semi-shaded position.

The right spot

A. flabellata positively prefers semi-shaded and moist conditions and is therefore a good subject for naturalizing in the woodland garden. The flowers of this charming plant are bell-shaped, with fluted petals in a delicate soft blue and short spurs. As it grows only to a height of 25cm/10in, it also makes it a suitable subject for a container.

There is also a white form, *A. f.* 'Nana Alba', which looks particularly handsome in the dappled shade of a woodland. Plant it in bold groups to get the best effect.

Rockeries make a good spot for aquilegias, although some may be too tall to fit comfortably into such a scheme. The alpine columbine (*A. alpina*) is one that should take to a rockery with ease. It is very hardy and reaches just 30cm/12in,

which is short for a columbine. The flowers of this pretty variety can be a clear blue or a more violet-blue shade. Be sure to provide a good, rich soil for it, as results will be disappointing unless it has plenty of nourishment.

An even smaller variety is *A. scopulorum,* which reaches a mere 6cm/2½in in height. It is less hardy than *A. alpina* but it will tolerate some frost. This is a pretty specimen with pale blue flowers, each with a cream centre. The petals have very long spurs.

Big and beautiful

However, it is with the larger varieties, such as the popular 'McKana Giant Hybrids', that the main charm of aquilegias lies. They make fine subjects for beds and herbaceous borders. The flowers are large, mostly bi-coloured and have long, slender spurs. The colours are glorious and include red, blue, cream, yellow, pink and white. They grow to a height of 75-90cm/2½-3ft, which makes them just right for planting in bold, colourful groups at the centre of an herbaceous border.

A. longissima is scented and has pale yellow blooms which boast very long, bright yellow spurs. A nice big clump of these would sit beautifully in a bed devoted to scented or aromatic plants. A sunny spot beneath a window or beside a

'McKana Giant Hybrids' (left) take the basic appeal of A. vulgaris and transform it into something considerably more exotic. The flowers – though not the plants themselves – are larger, generally bi-coloured, and have elegantly elongated spurs, and can make a colourful splash in the centre of a summer herbaceous border. At the other end of the size scale is the ground-hugging A. scopulorum (above), whose long-spurred flowers are just 6cm/2½in off the ground.

doorway is ideal for a perfumed garden, because the heavenly scents can drift into your home.

The original 'granny's bonnets' of old cottage gardens, the wild columbine (*A. vulgaris*) comes in several shades of pink, dark blue, crimson, white and purple. These are tall plants, around 90cm/3ft. 'Nora Barlow' has double, red flowers with pale green tips.

Cheap and cheeful

Although aquilegias are fairly short-lived, do not let this put you off; replacements are relatively simple and cheap to grow from seed.

Aquilegias flower in their second year, and the quality of the plants tends to deteriorate after this. Useful life may be prolonged by supplying plenty of leaf mould and peat at the time of planting so that the soil retains moisture and the young plants get plenty of nourishment. Regular dead-heading will ensure a succession of blooms so that you get the most out of your plants.

The best plan is to start off some new seeds as your previous batch become established in the garden. This will ensure that your beds and borders are graced with these exquisite flowers year in, year out.

Aquilegia seed may be sown at virtually any time. Some authorities suggest late winter or early spring, others recommend the autumn. Outdoor sowings can take place in summer when the soil is warm.

Successful sowing

For indoor sowing, simply fill trays with good seed compost and then water. Next, sprinkle seed over the surface. Do not cover the seeds with compost, as light is an essential ingredient for successful germination. It is important to keep seeds and seedlings moist if they are to thrive.

When the seedlings are large enough to handle, pot on. The seedlings may be planted out in spring or in autumn depending on the sowing time. If you are sowing in cold weather, in late winter or early spring, the seed trays should be kept on a warm window sill but away from direct sunlight.

Summer sowings may be made straight into the garden where you wish the plants to flower. Dig the ground over first and mix in some leaf mould and peat. Rake it over until the surface is fairly fine. Water the site and sprinkle your seeds across the surface. Be sure to keep the seed bed moist and thin the seedlings out if necessary.

White is part of the colour range of most aquilegia species and hybrids, but few are as purely coloured as 'Nana Alba' (left), a form of A. flabellata. Most hybrid forms are valued for the variety, rather than the purity, of their colouring. The blooms of 'Mrs Scott Elliott', for example, boast just about every colour in the columbine's range, often in spectacular bi-coloured versions (right).

WHAT'S IN A NAME?

The name aquilegia derives from the Latin *aquila*, an eagle. The spurs on the petals were supposed to resemble the bird's talons.

The common name has its origin in another image of birds, albeit a more gentle one. Columbine is from the Latin *columba*, a dove or pigeon. This is because of a supposed resemblance between the flowers and a flight of these birds. An older English name, culverwort, derives from the Saxon, and also means pigeon plant.

Index

Index *(continued)*

Picture Credits

Abbreviations: b = bottom; c = centre; i = inset; l = left; r = right; t = top.

J Bain/NHPA: page 86 (tr). Gillian Beckett: page 11 (bl); page 34 (tl); page 35 (br); page 54; page 73 (t & bl); page 75 (b); page 101 (tr & br); page 132 (t); page 138 (t); page 157 (b); page 159 (b); page 161 (t); page 163 (tr). Pat Brindley: page 3; page 4 (b); page 24 (t); page 26 (t); page 44; page 50 (b); page 61 (t); page 64 (t); page 65 (t); page 75 (t); page 92 (tl); page 109 (t); page 110 (l); page 112 (t); page 137 (t); page 138 (br); page 139 (br); page 142 (bl); page 164 (t). Chris Burrows/Garden Picture Library: page 130. Brian Carter/Garden Picture Library: page 99 (b); page 146; page 161 (b). Eric Crichton: cover (l); page 1; page 23 (t); page 29 (b); page 30 (b); page 31 (r); page 40 (b); page 41 (c); page 57 (b); page 60 (c); page 84 (b); page 86 (tl & br); page 96 (t); page 98 (b); page 102 (tl); page 110 (tr & br); page 118; page 119 (br); page 120 (tr); page 126 (b); page 129 (tr); page 132 (b); page 135 (t); page 136 (bi); page 142 (tr); page 147 (c); page 152 (t); page 159 (t); page 160; page 163 (br); page 170 (t); page 172 (b); page 173 (b). Collections/Patrick Johns: page 11 (t); page 22 (l); page 50 (t); page 66 (b); page 165. Bob Gibbons/Natural Image: page 99 (ti). John Glover: page 11 (tl); page 32 (t); page 36 (tl); page 164 (b). John Glover/Garden Picture Library: page 42 (b); page 59 (b); page 147 (t). Derek Gould: cover (tr); page 7 (t); page 49; page 53 (tl & tr); page 58 (r); page 79 (b); page 100 (tl); page 102 (br); page 106 (t); page 112 (b); page 149 (tl); page 157 (t); page 166 (t); page 167 (b). Marijke Heuff/Garden Picture Library: page 15-16 (c); page 42 (t); page 72; page 91 (l). Neil Holmes: page 15 (r); page 18 (tl); page 33; page 87 (br); page 153 (b). Insight Picture Library: page 36 (tr); page 55 (t); page 56 (t); page 73 (cr); page 92 (br); page 148 (tl). Lamontagne/Garden Picture Library: page 23 (b). Andrew Lawson: cover (bc); page 5; page 6 (t); page 11 (r); page 21 (bl); page 28 (t); page 31 (tl); page 32 (b); page 35 (tr); page 37 (tr); page 41 (t); page 76 (tl); page 84 (t); page 109 (c); page 116 (b); page 131 (br); page 133 (b); page 134 (t & b); page 135 (b); page 139 (tr); page 145 (tr); page 156 (t); page 158 (b). Peter McHoy: page 16 (cr); page 29 (t); page 58 (l); page 59 (t); page 61 (c); page 64 (b); page 70 (bc); page 100 (tr); page 113; page 114 (b); page 128 (b); page 144 (tl); page 148 (b); page 168 (tr). Marshall Cavendish: page 14 (b); page 16 (t & br); page 17 (br); page 18 (bc & r, & cl); page 21 (tr & cr); page 36 (bc & r); page 48 (t); page 56 (c); page 101 (bl); page 106 (b); page 107 (b); page 115 (tr & cr); page 143 (tr & b). Tania Midgley: page 13 (t & b); page 34 (bl); page 37 (br); page 48 (b); page 69 (b); page 74 (t); page 76 (tr); page 81 (t); page 93 (tr); page 103 (tr); page 114 (tr); page 116 (t); page 117 (b); page 136 (l); page 145 (b); page 168 (b). Sidney Moulds/Garden Picture Library: page 10 (b). Nature Photographers: page 93 (b). Clive Nicholas/Garden Picture Library: page 85 (t). Jerry Pavla/Garden Picture Library: page 19 (t). Photos Horticultural: page 4 (t); page 8 (b); page 9 (t & b); page 10 (t); page 12 (bl); page 16 (bl); page 19 (b); page 21 (br); page 24 (c); page 25 (b); page 27 (t); page 29 (c); page 34 (tr & br); page 38 (b); page 38-9 (b); page 45 (t & b); page 46 (t); page 47 (tr & b); page 62; page 63; page 66 (t); page 68 (t); page 70 (tc); page 74 (b); page 76 (b); page 78; page 80 (b); page 82 (t); page 88 (t); page 94 (br); page 95 (cr); page 97 (t & b); page 104 (ti); page 105 (bl); page 107 (t); page 108; page 114 (tl); page 119 (t); page 120 (tl); page 121 (bl); page 122 (tl & br); page 123 (br); page 124; page 125 (t & b); page 126 (t); page 127 (b); page 133 (t); page 140 (t); page 141 (b); page 150; page 151 (tr & cr); page 153 (b); page 154 (t); page 154 (b); page 156 (b); page 162 (t); page 167 (tl & tr); page 169 (tr); page 170 (b); page 172 (t). Stephen Robertson/Garden Picture Library: page 67 (b). Gary Rodgers/Garden Picture Library: page 177 (br). S & O Matthews: page 20 (t); page 41 (b); page 51 (t); page 52 (b); page 105 (br); page 141 (t); page 151 (b); page 158 (t). J S Sira/Garden Picture Library: page 131 (t); page 144 (tr). Harry Smith Collection: cover (br); page 6-7 (b); page 7 (br); page 8 (t); page 22 (r); page 24 (b); page 25 (c); page 26 (b); page 27 (t); page 28 (c); page 30 (t); page 31 (bl); page 39 (b); page 40 (t); page 43 (tr & br); page 51 (b); page 52 (t); page 53 (b); page 55 (b); page 56 (b); page 57 (t); page 60 (t & b); page 65 (b); page 67 (t); page 68 (b); page 69 (t); page 71 (tr & br); page 79 (t); page 80 (t); page 81 (b); page 83; page 85 (t); page 88 (bl); page 89 (br); page 90 (tl); page 91 (tr & br); page 94 (t); page 95 (t); page 96 (t); page 98 (t); page 100 (br); page 102 (bl); page 104 (l); page 109 (br); page 111 (br); page 117 (t); page 119 (bl); page 121 (tr); page 123 (tl); page 127 (t & c); page 128 (t); page 129 (t); page 131 (bl); page 137 (br); page 140 (b); page 144 (b); page 147 (b); page 155; page 162 (b); page 169 (b); page 171 (t & b); page 173 (t). Brigitte Thomas/Garden Picture Library: page 46 (b); page 105 (t). Don Wildbridge: page 77 (cr); page 82 (b); page 115 (br); page 154 (t).